JUNIOR
Encyclopedia

Miles Kelly

First published in 2016 by Miles Kelly Publishing Ltd
Harding's Barn, Bardfield End Green, Thaxted, Essex, CM6 3PX, UK

Copyright © Miles Kelly Publishing Ltd 2016

This edition printed 2019

6 8 10 9 7 5

Publishing Director Belinda Gallagher
Creative Director Jo Cowan
Editorial Director Rosie Neave
Senior Editor Sarah Parkin
Cover Designer Simon Lee
Senior Designer Rob Hale
Indexer Jane Parker
Production Elizabeth Collins, Jennifer Brunwin-Jones
Reprographics Stephan Davis, Callum Ratcliffe-Bingham
Assets Lorraine King

ISBN 978-1-78209-969-7

Printed in China

British Library Cataloguing-in-Publication Data
A catalogue record for this book is available from the British Library

Made with paper from a sustainable forest

www.mileskelly.net

CONTENTS

INCREDIBLE SPACE   6–21

Space is everywhere...... 6

Our life-giving star........8

The planet family 10

Earth in space 12

Rocky planets 14

Gassy planets 16

Birth of a star 18

The Milky Way 20

ACTIVE EARTH   22–37

How Earth was made 22

Changing rocks 24

Violent volcanoes....... 26

Making mountains 28

Extreme earthquakes.... 30

Lakes and rivers 32

Caves and chambers 34

Rivers of ice 36

WILD WEATHER   38–47

What is weather? 38

All the seasons 40

The water cycle......... 42

Windy weather 44

Thunder and lightning ... 46

SUPER SCIENCE   48–67

Our world of science 48

Hot science 50

Light at work.......... 52

What a noise! 54

Magnet power.......... 56

What is electricity? 58

Making sounds
and pictures.......... 60

Computer science....... 62

What is it made of? 64

Mini science........... 66

CONTENTS

DEADLY DINOSAURS 68–83

Early dinosaurs **68**

Gentle giants. **70**

Huge hunters. **72**

Super senses **74**

Slow or speedy? **76**

Baby dinosaurs **78**

Dinosaurs in battle. **80**

Where did they go? **82**

OCEAN LIFE 84–95

Ocean mammals. **84**

Ocean reptiles. **86**

Deep-sea creatures **88**

Super swimmers **90**

Fast flippers. **92**

Great travellers **94**

FANTASTIC MAMMALS 96–113

What are mammals? **96**

Baby mammals **98**

River mammals **100**

Snow mammals. **102**

Fins and flippers **104**

In the rainforest **106**

Desert life **108**

Plant food **110**

Hungry hunters. **112**

BRILLIANT BIRDS 114–131

What is a bird? **114**

Starting life **116**

Bird homes. **118**

Swimmers and divers . . . **120**

Feeding time **122**

Fierce hunters **124**

Rainforest birds. **126**

Snow birds **128**

River life. **130**

CONTENTS

AWESOME BUGS 132–147

What is a bug? **132**

The insect world **134**

Insect homes **136**

Taking flight **138**

Hop, skip and jump **140**

Dinner time **142**

What is a spider? **144**

All about legs **146**

ANCIENT EGYPT 148–159

Life on the Nile **148**

Powerful pharaohs **150**

The pyramids of Giza . . . **152**

Temples and tombs **154**

The working life **156**

Painting words **158**

ANCIENT ROME 160–171

The Roman Empire **160**

Rulers of Rome **162**

The people of Rome **164**

A trip to the baths **166**

The mighty Colosseum . . **168**

In the army **170**

KNIGHTS AND CASTLES 172–187

Life in the Middle Ages . . **172**

Building castles **174**

Inside the castle **176**

Nobles and knights **178**

Jousting tournaments . . **180**

Into battle **182**

Castle siege **184**

Fighting back **186**

INDEX 188

ACKNOWLEDGEMENTS 192

Space is everywhere

Space is all around Earth, high above the air. Here on Earth's surface we are surrounded by air. If you go upwards, up a mountain or in an aircraft, air grows thinner until there is none at all. This is where space begins.

Rocky ring
Asteroids are chunks of rock, which are part of our Solar System. They circle the Sun in a ring, between the planets Mars and Jupiter. This is called the asteroid belt.

Create your own space city

You will need
cardboard box • foil • scissors • glue
empty containers — plastic bottles, cardboard tubes,
cans, yoghurt pots and lids

1 Use the lid of the box as your base and cover it
with foil. Cover all the empty containers with
foil, too.

2 Cut plastic bottles to make domes. Use tubes and
cans to make tunnels and passages, and lids to
make satellite dishes.

3 Stick everything to the base and play with your
own space city!

Astronauts are people
who travel in space.

The surface of **Earth** is
made up of land and
water — the oceans
and seas.

Rockets are so powerful
that they can launch
spacecraft into space.

Our life-giving star

The Sun is our nearest star. To us, it does not look like other stars because it is much closer to Earth. The Sun is not solid like Earth — it is a giant ball of super-hot gases.

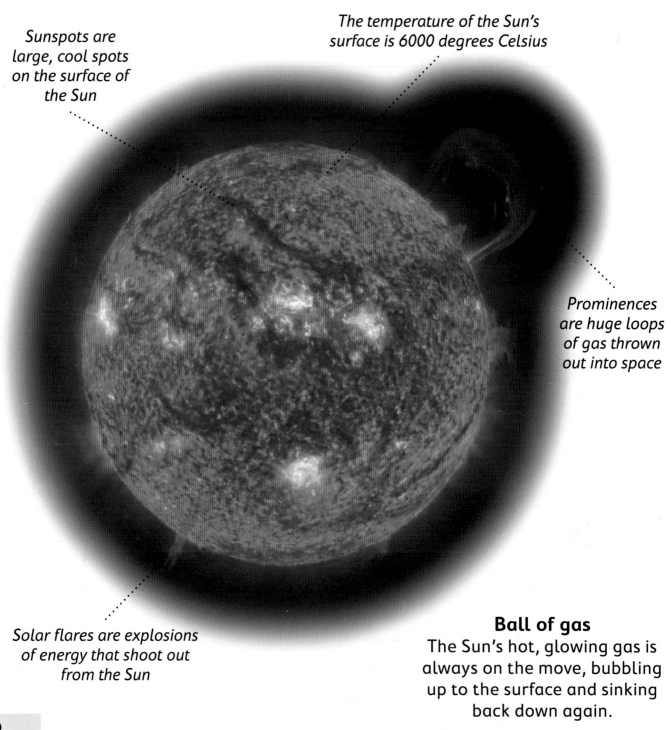

Sunspots are large, cool spots on the surface of the Sun

The temperature of the Sun's surface is 6000 degrees Celsius

Prominences are huge loops of gas thrown out into space

Solar flares are explosions of energy that shoot out from the Sun

Ball of gas
The Sun's hot, glowing gas is always on the move, bubbling up to the surface and sinking back down again.

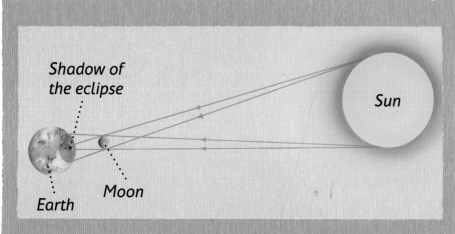

Shadow of the eclipse

Sun

Earth

Moon

Solar eclipse

Every so often, the Sun, Moon and Earth line up in space so that the Moon is directly between Earth and the Sun. This stops sunlight from reaching a small area on Earth. The area grows dark and cold, as if night-time has come early. This is called an eclipse.

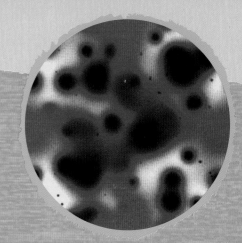

Sunspots appear as dark patches on the Sun's surface. They may be 1500 degrees Celsius cooler than other areas.

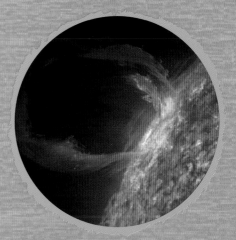

Solar prominences can be huge, with some reaching up to 100,000 kilometres into space.

Blackout

When the Moon completely covers the Sun, it is called a total eclipse. All that can be seen is the Sun's corona, a ring of white glowing gas. Although the Moon and the Sun look the same size in an eclipse, the Sun is actually 400 times bigger than the Moon, and 400 times further away.

FUN FACT!

The surface of the Sun is nearly 60 times hotter than boiling water. It is so hot, it would melt a spacecraft that flew near it.

The planet family

The Sun is surrounded by a family of eight circling planets called the Solar System. This family is held together by an invisible force called gravity, which pulls things towards each other. It is the same force that pulls us to the ground and stops us floating away.

Big and small
The eight planets are all different. Mercury, nearest to the Sun, is small and hot. Venus, Earth and Mars are rocky and cooler. Beyond them Jupiter, Saturn, Uranus and Neptune are large and cold.

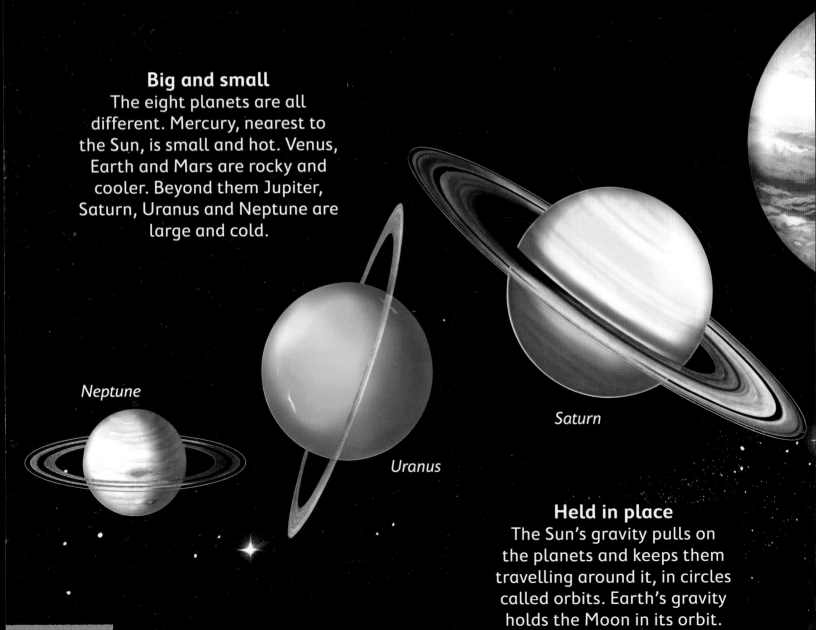

Neptune

Uranus

Saturn

Held in place
The Sun's gravity pulls on the planets and keeps them travelling around it, in circles called orbits. Earth's gravity holds the Moon in its orbit.

Sun

Mercury

Moon

Venus

Jupiter

Earth

Mars

Some planets have **rings** made of ice, dust and rocks. Saturn is famous for its rings.

Some planets have **swirling atmospheres** of gas.

Make a mobile

You will need
card • scissors • colouring pencils • string
paper plate • sticky tape

1 Cut out nine circles of card, some big and some small, to be the planets and the Sun.

2 Colour the circles to look like the Sun and planets.

3 Use string and tape to hang the circles around the outside of the plate.

4 Hang your mobile from string stuck to the other side of the plate.

Earth in space

Earth orbits the Sun at nearly 30,000 metres a second. It weighs 6000 million, million, million tonnes. Up to two thirds of Earth's rocky surface is covered by water, making the seas and oceans.

Craters are made when rocks crash into the Moon's surface

Dark areas are low, flat plains called seas

The Moon

Most planets have moons circling around them. Earth's Moon is one of the largest in the Solar System. Scientists think the Moon was formed over three billion years ago.

Venus

Mercury

Sun

Moon

Earth

Galaxies are giant groups of millions or even trillions of stars.

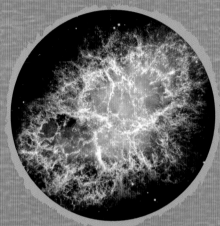

A cloud of dust and gas in space is called a **nebula.**

Bulging planet
Earth is the fifth largest planet in the Solar System. As it spins in space, Earth bulges in the middle, like a pumpkin.

Our atmosphere

Surrounding Earth is a layer of gases called the atmosphere. It stretches 700 kilometres from Earth's surface.

A **star** is a ball of very hot gas.

Rocky planets

Four rocky planets orbit closest to the Sun. Mercury has no atmosphere, so it is very hot in the day and freezing at night. Venus orbits between Mercury and Earth. It is a similar size to Earth, and hotter than Mercury. Mars is the furthest of the rocky planets from the Sun. Its surface is dry and reddish in colour.

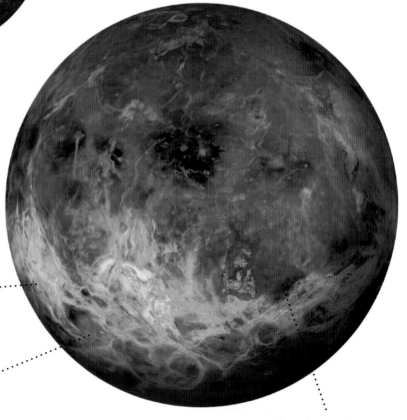

The dusty surface is covered in craters

Mercury

Mercury has many craters. This shows how often it was hit by space rocks. One was so large, it shattered rocks on the other side of the planet.

With no air to hold heat, Mercury's temperature may drop below −170 degrees Celsius at night

Venus

Venus shines like a star in the sky because its atmosphere reflects sunlight so well.

Poisonous clouds with drops of acid

Venus is the hottest planet because its clouds trap the heat

Rocky surface

Earth

The third planet from the Sun has water and air — both of which living things need to survive, so all kinds of animals and plants can thrive here.

Earth has seven continents (land masses) and five oceans

From space, Earth has been likened to a beautiful marble, with its deep blue oceans and swirling white clouds

The Sun looks huge as it rises over Mercury.

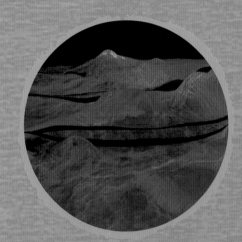

Venus has a volcano called **Maat Mons**. It is 6 kilometres high.

Mars

Mars is very dry, like a desert. Winds whip up huge dust storms that can cover the whole planet.

White ice caps are made of frozen carbon dioxide gas

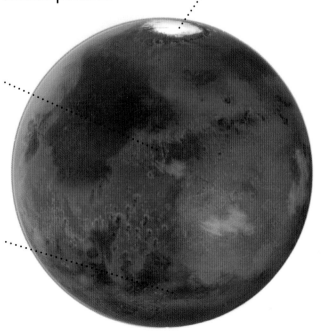

The surface of Mars is covered in a reddish dust

The southern hemisphere has many craters and large canyons

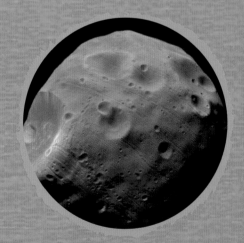

Mars has two small moons. **Phobos** is only 27 kilometres across.

15

Gassy planets

The four outer planets are almost entirely made of gas. Jupiter is the largest planet in the Solar System, at 11 times wider than Earth. Saturn, the next largest, is famous for its icy rings. Beyond Saturn, Uranus and Neptune are much smaller – less than half as wide.

Jupiter

There are many storms on Jupiter, but none as large or long lasting as the Great Red Spot.

Different-coloured clouds stretch around Jupiter

Yellow clouds stretch to make faint bands

The Great Red Spot is a 300-year-old storm

Saturn's shining rings are made of millions of chunks of ice

Saturn

From Earth, Saturn looks like a faint but bright-yellow star in the sky.

Jupiter has a moon called **Io**. It has many active volcanoes.

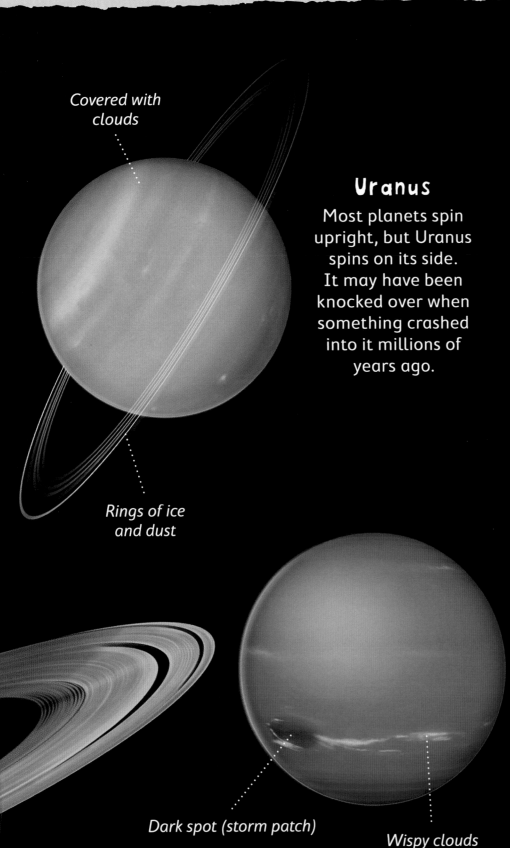

Covered with clouds

Rings of ice and dust

Uranus

Most planets spin upright, but Uranus spins on its side. It may have been knocked over when something crashed into it millions of years ago.

The **Galilean moons** are Jupiter's four biggest moons. They were discovered by Italian astronomer Galileo Galilei.

Dark spot (storm patch)

Wispy clouds

Neptune

The strongest winds in the Solar System blow icy clouds around Neptune.

Neptune's **bright blue clouds** make the whole planet look blue.

17

Birth of a star

A star is born in clouds of dust and gas called nebulae. These clouds look like shining patches in the night sky. They shrink as gravity pulls the dust and gas together. At the centre, the gas gets hotter until a new star is born.

Learning about stars
Stars are born and die across the Universe all the time. By looking at stars in the different stages of their lives, astonomers have learned how they work.

1 *Clumps of gas in the nebula start to shrink into tight balls that will become stars*

2 *The gas spirals as it is pulled inwards. Any leftover gas and dust may form planets around the new star*

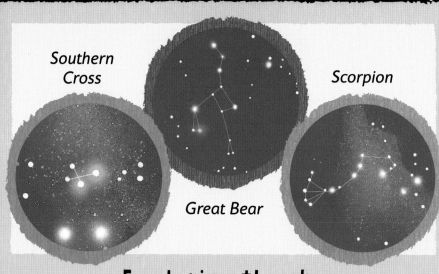

Southern Cross

Scorpion

Great Bear

Exploring the sky

Outlines of people and animals in star patterns in the sky are called constellations. Astronomers named the constellations to help them find their way around the skies.

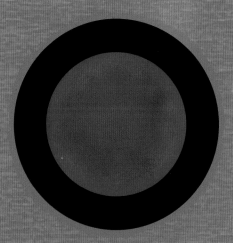

Large **white stars** make energy very quickly and burn brightly.

Small **red stars** are cooler and shine less brightly.

3 *Deep in its centre, the new star starts making energy, but it is still hidden by the cloud of dust and gas*

4 *The dust and gas are blown away and the star shines*

The Sun has existed for five billion years — only half its life.

The Milky Way

The Sun is part of a huge family of stars called the Milky Way galaxy. There are billions of other stars in the galaxy and there are also billions of galaxies outside the Milky Way.

Our galaxy
The arms at the edge of the Milky Way contain young, bright stars. The centre of the Milky Way is made of dust and gas.

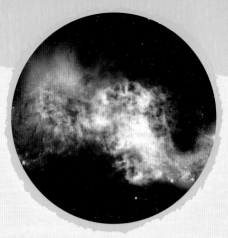

Irregular galaxies don't have a particular shape.

Collision!

Galaxies sometimes get so close to each other that they collide. When this happens, they may pull each other out of shape, or merge into one larger galaxy.

Spiral galaxies have arms made of bright stars, like our Milky Way.

FUN FACT!

Our galaxy is called the Milky Way because it looks like a faint band of light in the sky, as though milk has been spilt across space.

Elliptical galaxies are shaped like a huge squashed ball.

How Earth was made

When an old star explodes, the remains create clouds of gas and dust. In these clouds, new stars and planets form. Earth came from a huge cloud of gas and dust about 4500 million years ago.

The birth of Earth
A star exploded near a cloud of gas and dust, making the cloud spin. Gases gathered at the centre of the cloud, forming the Sun. Rocks crashed into each other, creating the planets. Earth is one of these planets.

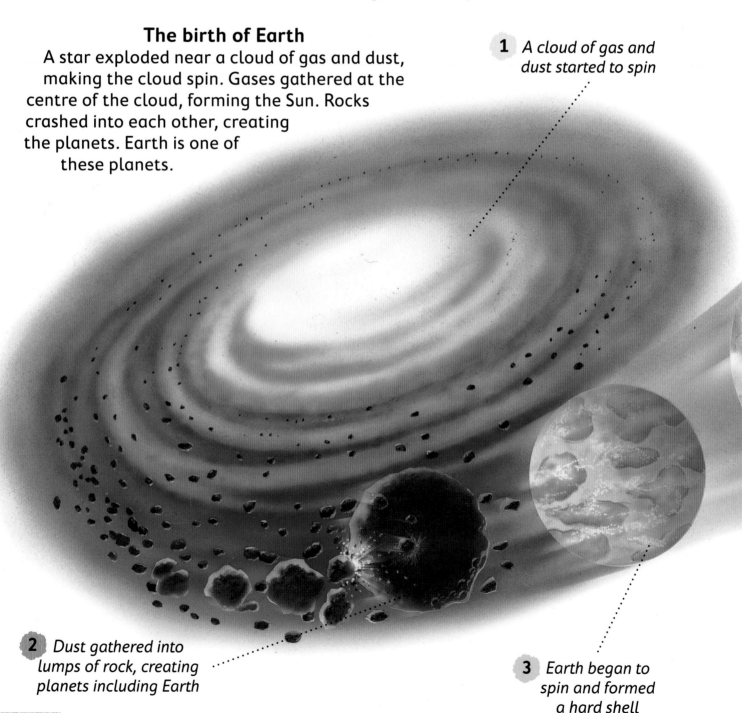

1 *A cloud of gas and dust started to spin*

2 *Dust gathered into lumps of rock, creating planets including Earth*

3 *Earth began to spin and formed a hard shell*

5 *Earth was first made up of one piece of land, but it has now split into seven chunks called continents*

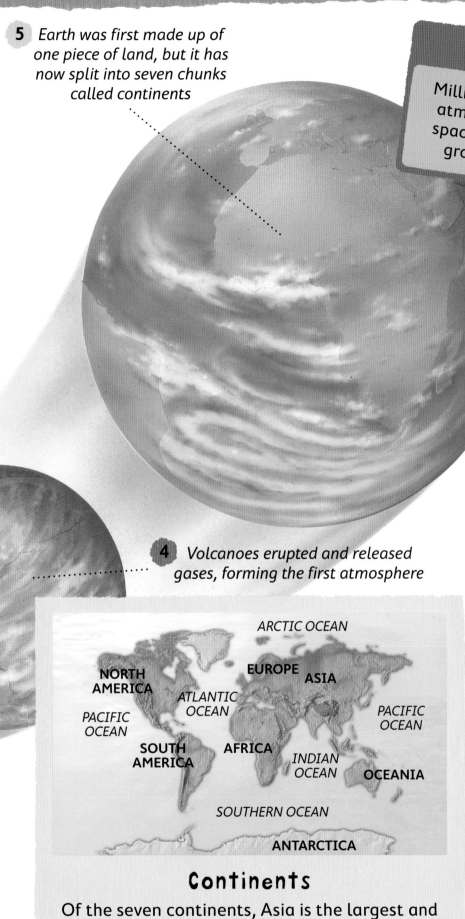

4 *Volcanoes erupted and released gases, forming the first atmosphere*

The surfaces of Earth and the **Moon** were hit by rocks, making hollows called craters.

ARCTIC OCEAN

NORTH AMERICA

EUROPE ASIA

ATLANTIC OCEAN

PACIFIC OCEAN

PACIFIC OCEAN

SOUTH AMERICA

AFRICA

INDIAN OCEAN

OCEANIA

SOUTHERN OCEAN

ANTARCTICA

Continents

Of the seven continents, Asia is the largest and Oceania the smallest. The Pacific is the biggest of the five oceans; the Arctic Ocean the smallest.

Meteor Crater is near Arizona, USA. It is 1200 metres wide and 170 metres deep.

Changing rocks

When rocks form in Earth's crust, they can change. This happens in two ways. Sometimes the rock is heated by hot rocks moving up through the crust. Other times, the crust is squashed and heated, and mountains form.

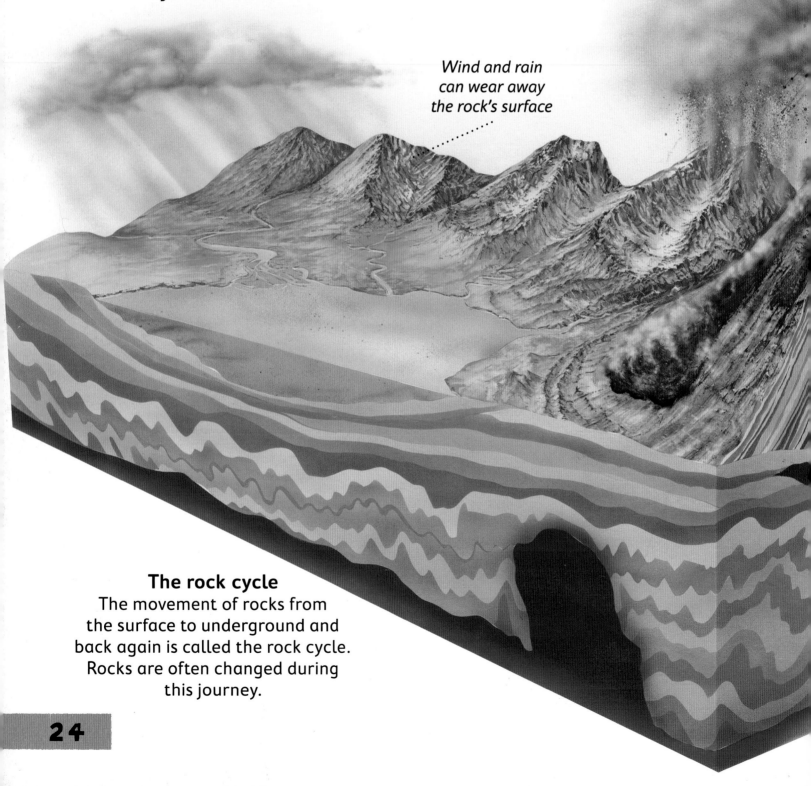

Wind and rain can wear away the rock's surface

The rock cycle
The movement of rocks from the surface to underground and back again is called the rock cycle. Rocks are often changed during this journey.

Inner core

Outer core

Lower mantle

Upper mantle

Continental crust

Inside Earth

Earth is made up of many different layers.
We live on the outer layer — the thin, rocky crust
that is covered with land and water.

Hot rock travels to
the surface through
the pipe in a volcano

Rock can become
squashed, causing
it to fold together

Rock melts, forming hot,
liquid rock called magma

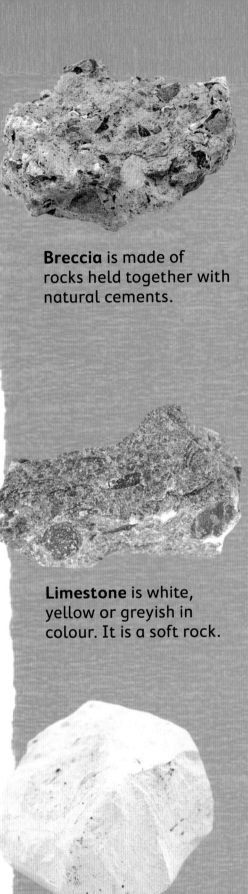

Breccia is made of
rocks held together with
natural cements.

Limestone is white,
yellow or greyish in
colour. It is a soft rock.

Chalk is a soft rock
that formed millions
of years ago.

Violent volcanoes

Volcanoes occur when hot, liquid rock shoots up through Earth's surface. Beneath a volcano is a huge space filled with molten (liquid) rock. This is the magma chamber. Eruptions happen when pressure builds up inside the chamber.

Volcanic explosion
When a volcano erupts, the hot rock from inside Earth escapes as ash, smoke, flying lava bombs and rivers of lava.

Lava bomb

Layers of rock from previous eruptions

Make an erupting volcano

You will need
bicarbonate of soda • plastic bottle
tray • sand • red food colouring • vinegar

1 With help from a grown-up, put a tablespoon of bicarbonate of soda in the plastic bottle.

2 Stand the bottle on a tray and make a cone of sand around it.

3 Put a few drops of red food colouring in half a cup of vinegar.

4 Pour the vinegar into the bottle and watch your volcano erupt!

Main vent

Lava flowing away from vent

Ash and smoke

Magma chamber beneath volcano

Shield volcanoes form when lava flows from the vent creating a dome shape.

Cone-shaped volcanoes form when ash settles on thick lava.

Crater volcanoes form when cone-shaped volcanoes sink into magma chambers.

27

Making mountains

It takes millions of years for mountains to form. Young mountains are the highest, but the peaks are made of soft rocks so they break down easily. Underneath are harder rocks that wear away over a longer period of time.

Volcanic mountains
These mountains are formed when lava erupts through Earth's crust. As the lava cools, it creates a rocky layer.

Active volcano

Mountain range is pushed up

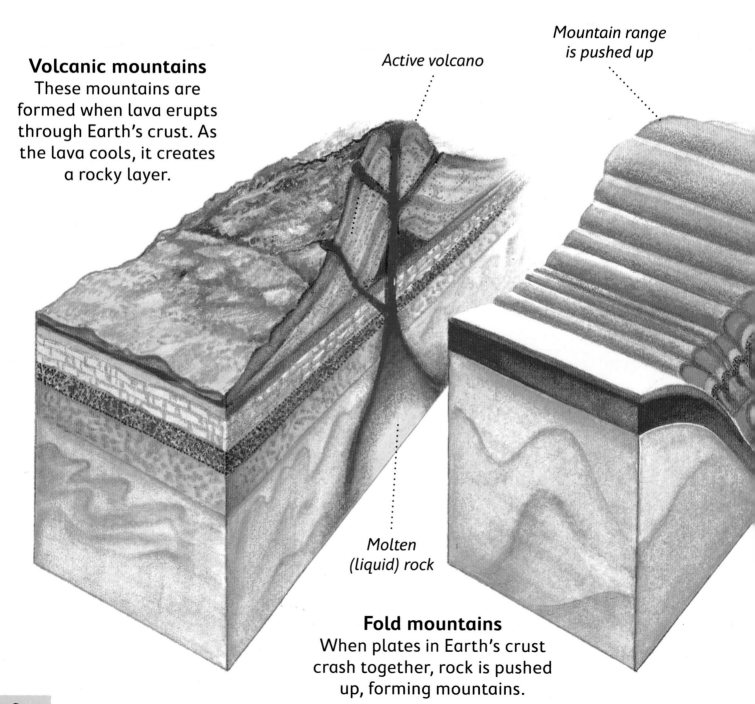

Molten (liquid) rock

Fold mountains
When plates in Earth's crust crash together, rock is pushed up, forming mountains.

Highest peaks
Some mountaintops are so high that they sit above the clouds.

Some **mountain peaks** are covered in snow.

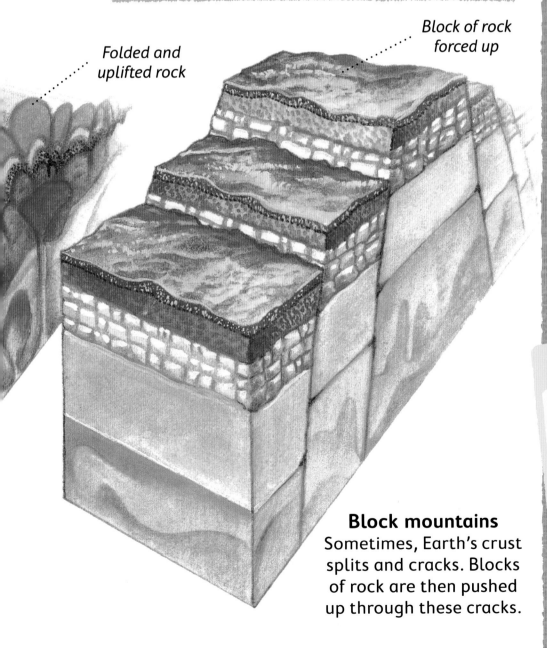

Folded and uplifted rock

Block of rock forced up

Mountaineers are people who like to climb mountains.

FUN FACT!

The highest mountain in the world is Mount Everest, which is part of the Himalayas. It is 8848 metres tall.

Block mountains
Sometimes, Earth's crust splits and cracks. Blocks of rock are then pushed up through these cracks.

Extreme earthquakes

An earthquake is caused by movements in Earth's crust. It starts deep underground at the focus. Shockwaves move from the focus in all directions, shaking the rock. The quake is strongest at the epicentre.

Locking plates

Earth's crust is made of plates and some of them have jagged edges. Sometimes they lock together – when they suddenly unlock, it can cause an earthquake.

The fault line is where two plates rub together

Tsunami hits

As the giant wave moves into shallow water near the coast, it becomes taller. It then crashes onto the shore, flooding the land.

A **fault line** can be made up of narrow cracks or deep canyons.

The epicentre is where the shockwaves reach the surface, directly above the focus

Shockwaves from an earthquake can create a giant wave at sea called a tsunami

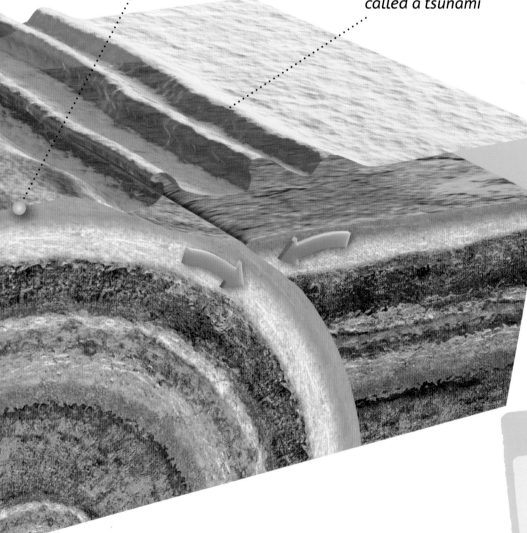

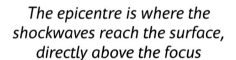

The force of an earthquake is measured using the **Richter scale**. At level 7, buildings collapse and cities can be destroyed.

The focus is deep underground – this is where the earthquake starts

FUN FACT!

The biggest earthquake ever recorded was near Valdivia, Chile, in May 1960. It measured 9.5 on the Richter scale.

Lakes and rivers

A mighty river can start from a small spring, where water flows from the ground. The trickle of water from a spring is called a stream. When streams join together, they make a river.

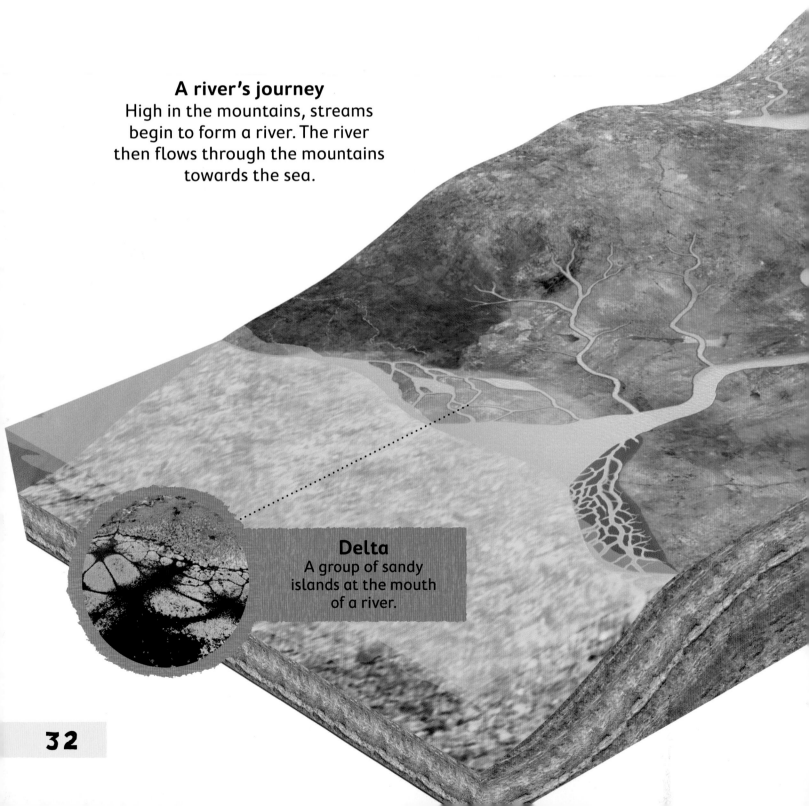

A river's journey
High in the mountains, streams begin to form a river. The river then flows through the mountains towards the sea.

Delta
A group of sandy islands at the mouth of a river.

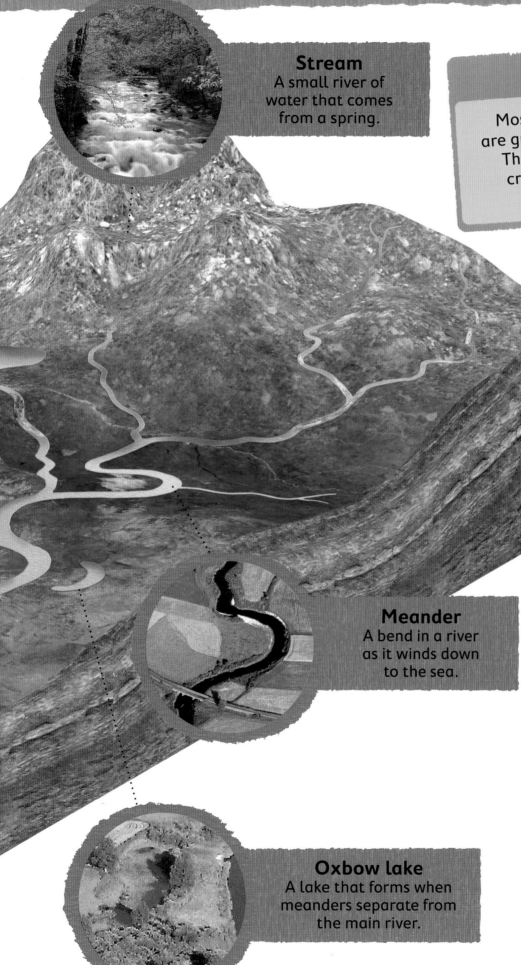

Stream
A small river of water that comes from a spring.

Meander
A bend in a river as it winds down to the sea.

Oxbow lake
A lake that forms when meanders separate from the main river.

FUN FACT!

Most lakes are blue, but some are green, pink, red or even white. The colours are made by tiny creatures called algae or by minerals in the water.

A **waterfall** forms when a river flows over a ledge.

A **lake** is a large body of water surrounded by land.

33

Caves and chambers

Rocks can be worn away by rainwater trickling into tiny cracks and crevices. Over millions of years, this creates caves, chambers and waterfalls underground.

Stalactites and stalagmites

Stalagmites grow up from the floor of caves and stalactites grow down from the roof. Over time, they can join together. They are made of the minerals in water.

34

Dissolving rock

Rainwater contains chemicals that can turn it into a weak acid. Acidic rainwater can slowly dissolve rock, especially limestone, when it trickles through any cracks.

FUN FACT!

The largest cave in the world is the Sarawak Chamber in Malaysia. At 600 metres long and 400 metres wide, you could fit eight Boeing 747 aeroplanes inside it.

Waterfall in a shaft (vertical cave)

Gallery (horizontal cave)

Stalactites

Stalagmites

Caves have been discovered full of **crystals**. The crystals are made of minerals.

Some spectacular **cave formations** are thousands of years old.

Rivers of ice

Glaciers are huge areas of ice that form near mountaintops. They slide slowly down the mountainside and melt. As a glacier moves, some rocks break off and are carried along.

Area where the glacier forms

Cracks in the ice

Melting ice
The end of a glacier is called the 'snout'. This is where the ice starts to melt, causing large chunks called icebergs to break off into the ocean.

Beautiful **U-shaped valleys** were created by glaciers.

Make an iceberg

You will need
small plastic container • water • clear bowl

1 Fill the container with water and put it in the freezer until it is frozen. This is your iceberg.

2 Remove the iceberg from the container. Fill the clear bowl with water and add your iceberg.

3 Look through the side of the container to see how much of your iceberg is underwater and what shape it makes.

Glacier valleys

Glaciers have helped to shape Earth. As a glacier flows down a mountain, the heavy ice pushes and scrapes the soil and rocks. This carves a huge U-shaped valley.

Glacial ice melts and crashes into the sea.

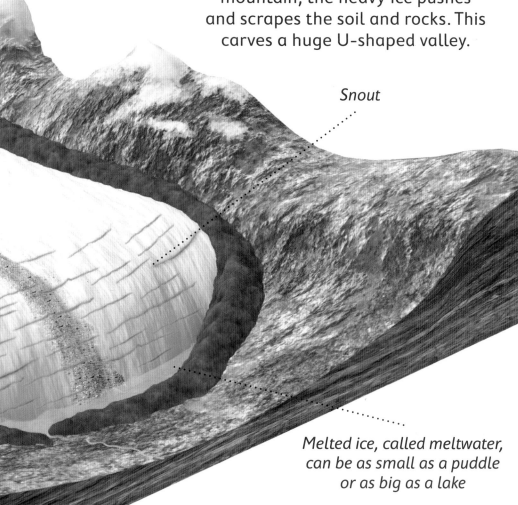

Snout

Melted ice, called meltwater, can be as small as a puddle or as big as a lake

Mushroom stones can be formed when glaciers cut away the bottom part of the rock.

What is weather?

Rain, sunshine and snow are all types of weather. In parts of the world, such as near the Equator, the weather is nearly always the same. Most of the world has a temperate climate, meaning the weather changes daily.

The world's climates
The coloured rings show the different climates around the world. In general, the warmest climates are found close to the Equator.

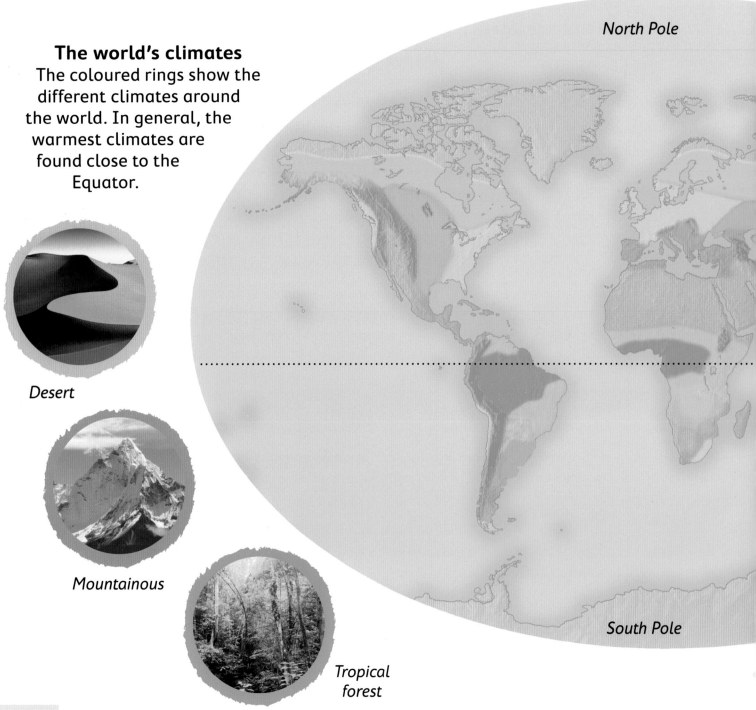

North Pole

South Pole

Desert

Mountainous

Tropical forest

Polar climates
The coldest climates in the world are found at the North and South Poles. They are furthest from the Equator, and so it is cold and icy all year round.

Rainforests are very hot but they also have daily downpours of rain.

Tropical grassland

Temperate grassland

Polar

Mountains can be very cold and covered in snow.

Equator

Wet temperate

Dry temperate

Cold temperate

Deserts are home to many plants and animals, such as lizards, that can survive in the heat.

All the seasons

The seasons are caused by Earth's movement around the Sun. It takes one year for Earth to orbit the Sun. Earth is tilted, so over the year the North and South Poles take turns facing towards the Sun, giving us seasons.

Spring in the Northern Hemisphere (March–May)
The temperature begins to get warmer. Flowers bloom, and trees start to grow their leaves again.

N

S

Sun

N

S

Summer in the Northern Hemisphere (June–September)
In June, the North Pole leans towards the Sun. The Sun heats the northern half of Earth, making it summertime.

Sunshine at midnight

At the North Pole during the height of summer, the Sun never disappears below the horizon.

In **summer**, people like to enjoy the sunshine by going to the beach.

In **winter**, many people go skiing and snowboarding in the snow.

N

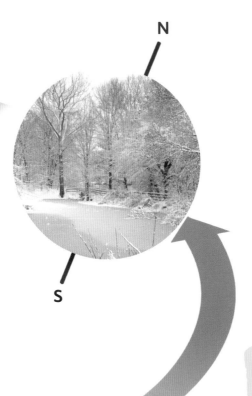

S

Winter in the Northern Hemisphere (December–March)
In December, the North Pole leans away from the Sun, meaning it is winter.

N

S

Autumn in the Northern Hemisphere (October–November)
In autumn, many forests change colour, from green to golden brown, as trees prepare to lose their leaves.

FUN FACT!

In Stockholm, Sweden, daylight on Midsummer's Day lasts for 21 hours – the Sun disappears below the horizon for just three hours!

The water cycle

The water cycle involves all the water on Earth. Water vapour rises from lakes, rivers and the sea to form clouds in the atmosphere.

Water, water, everywhere

Too much rain causes flooding. Flash floods happen after a short burst of heavy rainfall.

1 *Water evaporates (disappears into the air) from the sea*

5 *The rivers run back to the sea, and the cycle starts again*

From sea to sky
As the Sun heats the ocean's surface, some water turns into water vapour (a kind of gas) and rises into the air to form clouds. Rain falls from the clouds, some of which is soaked up by the land, but a lot finds its way back to the sea.

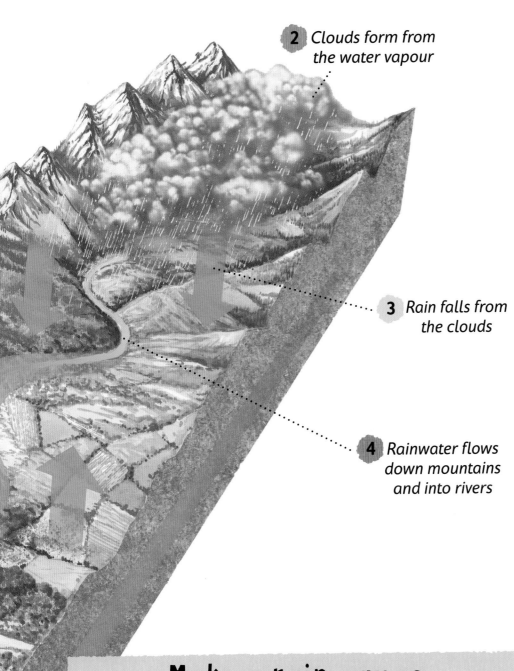

2 *Clouds form from the water vapour*

3 *Rain falls from the clouds*

4 *Rainwater flows down mountains and into rivers*

Cumulonimbus clouds give heavy rain showers.

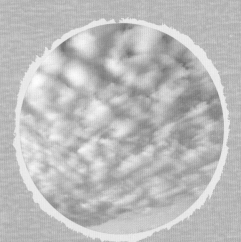

Stratus clouds can bring drizzle or appear as fog.

Cirrus clouds look like wisps of smoke. They are unlikely to bring rain.

Make a rain gauge

You will need
jar • marker pen • ruler • notebook • pen

1 Place the jar outside where it can collect rain.

2 Use the marker pen to mark the water level on the outside of the jar each day.

3 Keep a record of the changing levels of rainfall in a notebook.

Windy weather

Wind is moving air. Winds blow because air is constantly moving from areas of high pressure to areas of low pressure. The bigger the difference in temperature between the two areas, the faster the wind blows.

Beaufort Scale

Wind strength is measured on the Beaufort Scale. The scale ranges from Force 0, meaning calm, to Force 12, which is a hurricane.

Calm
Chimney smoke rises straight up

Light air
Smoke drifts gently

Near gale
Whole trees start to sway

Fresh breeze
Small trees sway

Gentle breeze
Washing flutters

Light breeze
Leaves rustle

Moderate breeze
Paper blows around

Strong breeze
Hard to control an umbrella

Gale
Difficult to walk into wind

A **hurricane** is a violent tropical storm with very fast winds.

Wind power

Wind turbines can be used to make electricity. As the wind turns each turbine, the movement powers a generator and produces electricity.

A cloud of dust and gas in space is called a **nebula.**

Severe gale
Small branches, tiles and chimneys are blown off

9

Severe storm
Serious damage

11

12

10

Storm
Houses damaged; trees blown down

Hurricane
Widespread damage

FUN FACT!

A tropical storm that starts in the Atlantic Ocean is called a hurricane. In the Pacific, it is called a typhoon. In the Indian Ocean it is a cyclone.

Thunder and lightning

Inside a big thundercloud, water drops and bits of ice move up and down, bumping into each other. This makes electricity build up. When the electricity jumps around, we see a spark of lightning and hear a loud clap of thunder.

Colours of lightning

Lightning comes in different colours. If there is rain in the thundercloud, the lightning looks red. If there's hail in the thundercloud, the lightning looks blue.

How close is the storm?

Thunder and lightning happen at the same time, but light travels faster than sound, so you see the lightning first.

1 When you see a lightning flash, count the seconds between the flash and the thunderclap that follows.

2 Then divide the number of seconds by three. This shows you how many kilometres away the storm is.

3 Keep a record and see if the storm moves closer or further away.

Sheet lightning travels from cloud to cloud.

Forked lightning travels from a cloud to the ground.

Hailstones
Hailstones are chunks of ice that fall from thunderclouds.

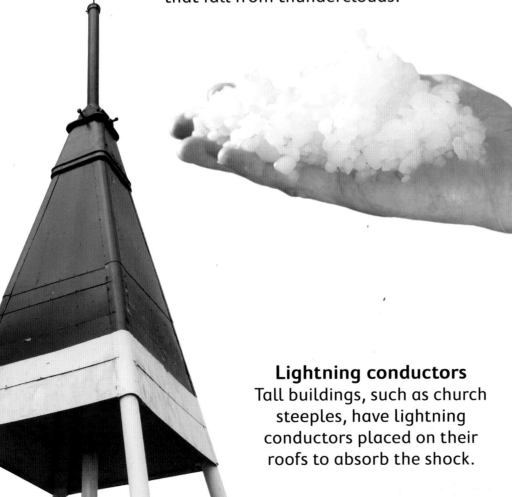

FUN FACT!
A person can survive a lightning strike. Lightning is very dangerous and can kill you, but American Roy Sullivan survived being struck seven times.

Lightning conductors
Tall buildings, such as church steeples, have lightning conductors placed on their roofs to absorb the shock.

Our world of science

Science is all around us. Toasters, bicycles, mobile phones, cars, computers, light bulbs — all the gadgets and machines we use every day are the result of scientific discoveries.

Feeling forces

Pushes and pulls make things stop and start. Scientists use the word 'force' for pushes and pulls. Forces are all around us. The force of gravity pulls things downwards. It makes a rollercoaster car hurtle downhill.

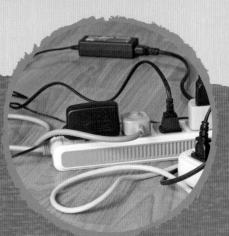

Hidden strength

Skyscrapers stay up because they have a strong frame on the inside. The frame is made from steel and concrete. These are very strong materials. The frame is hidden by the skyscraper's walls.

Electricity is a type of energy that makes lots of things around us work.

We have **transport** like cars, trains and planes because of scientific discoveries.

Space exploration is a type of science.

49

Hot science

Heat is important in many ways. We cook with heat, warm our homes and heat water. Even factories use heat to make products, such as plastic toys.

Fizz! Crackle! Bang! Fireworks flash and bang because they are full of chemicals that burn. The chemicals have lots of energy stored in them. When they burn, the energy changes to light, heat and sound.

How candles burn

When the candle wick is lit, the wax around it melts. The wick soaks up the liquid wax and the heat of the flame turns the wax into a gas (vapour), which burns away. As the wax becomes vapour it cools the wick, allowing the candle to burn slowly.

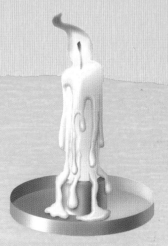

Hot air rises from a candle. This movement of heat is called **convection**.

A hot drink passes its heat to the spoon, warming it up. Heat moves by **conduction**.

Carrying heat

You will need
frozen peas • butter • wooden ruler
metal spoon • plastic spatula • heatproof jug

1 Fix a frozen pea with butter to the end of the ruler, spoon and spatula.

2 Put the other ends in a heatproof jug. Ask an adult to fill the jug with hot water.

3 Heat is conducted (passed on) from the water, up the object, to melt the butter. Which object is the best conductor?

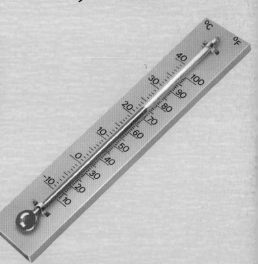

A thermometer is used for measuring heat.

Light at work

Light is energy that you can see. Light waves are tiny. About 2000 of them laid end to end would stretch across this full stop.

Splitting light

Light rays travel in straight lines. When light shines through a prism, the rays bend. When sunlight (white light) passes through a prism it splits into many colours, like a rainbow.

Prism

Spectrum

White light

Colours of the rainbow

Red
Orange
Yellow
Green
Blue
Indigo
Violet

Bouncing light

Light waves bounce off surfaces that are smooth, such as a mirror. This is called reflection.

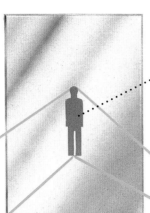

Reflection

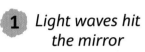

1 *Light waves hit the mirror*

2 *Light is directed back so you see a back-to-front reflection*

As light passes through a glass of water, it **refracts** (bends) and makes the straw look bent.

Shades of colour

You will need
different-coloured paints
paintbrush • pen • paper

1 Mix two different colours of paint together.

2 Write down what colours you mix and what colour they make.

3 Paint a picture using your new colours.

Cameras make pictures by using lenses and light.

What a noise!

Listening to the radio or television depends on the science of sound. Sounds are carried by invisible waves in the air, which travel about 330 metres per second. This is one million times slower than light waves.

Atom bomb 210 dB

Thunder 100 dB

Talking 40 dB

The decibel scale
Scientists measure the loudness of sound in decibels (dB). One of the loudest sounds that we hear is a jet plane engine.

Jet taking off 140 dB

Rustling leaves 10 dB

Making the journey

We cannot see sound waves but we can hear them using our ears. Sound waves travel through our ears to our brain.

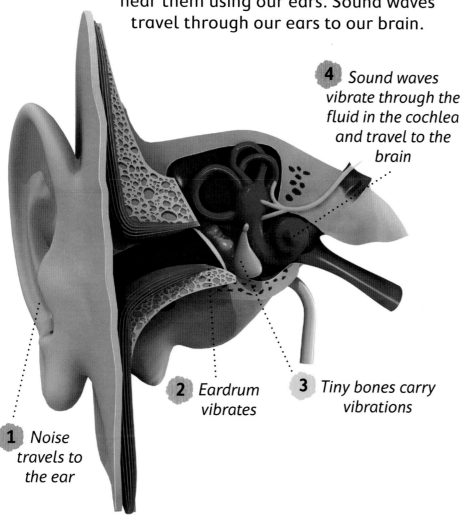

4 *Sound waves vibrate through the fluid in the cochlea and travel to the brain*

2 *Eardrum vibrates*

3 *Tiny bones carry vibrations*

1 *Noise travels to the ear*

FUN FACT!

Sound waves bounce off hard, flat surfaces. This is called an echo.

Loudspeakers change electrical signals into sound waves.

When you speak, **sound waves** spread out so everyone can hear what you say.

Box guitar

You will need
shoebox • split pins • elastic band

1 Cut a hole about 10 centimetres across on one side of an empty shoebox.

2 Push split pins through either side of the hole, and stretch an elastic band between them.

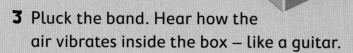

3 Pluck the band. Hear how the air vibrates inside the box — like a guitar.

Magnet power

Magnetism is an invisible force that pulls things together or pushes them apart. Magnets are made from lumps of iron or steel. You can turn a piece of iron into a magnet by stroking it with another magnet.

Magnetic machine
A magnet can also be made by sending electricity through a coil of wire. This is called an electromagnet. Some electromagnets are so strong, they can pick up cars.

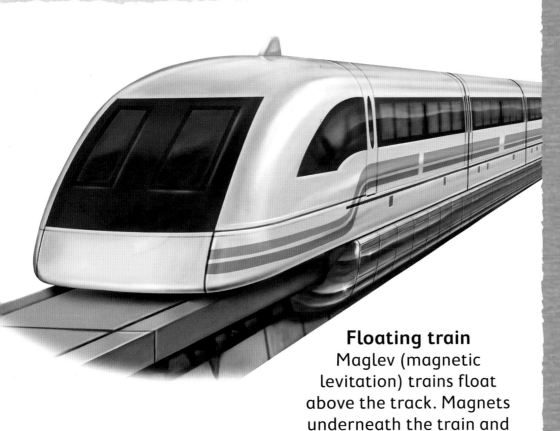

A magnet has two different **poles** — north and south.

Floating train
Maglev (magnetic levitation) trains float above the track. Magnets underneath the train and in the track repel (push) each other.

Electromagnets are so strong they can lift whole cars.

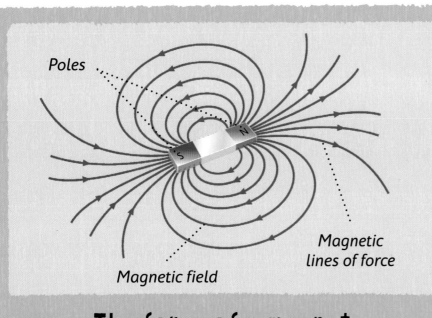

Poles

Magnetic field

Magnetic lines of force

The force of a magnet
A magnet is a block of iron or steel. A force surrounds the magnet, in a region called the magnetic field. The magnetic field is strongest at the two parts of the magnet called the poles.

A car's body is made from **iron-based steel**, which is magnetic.

What is electricity?

Electricity is energy that flows from a power station to our homes. It is used all around us to power washing machines, vacuum cleaners and kettles. Electricity is made by the movement of electrons inside atoms.

Hopping electrons
When electrons are 'pushed', they hop from one atom to the next. This is how electricity flows.

Electron

Atom

Checking cables

Electricity from power stations is carried along cables on high pylons. It is very powerful and extremely dangerous. When cables need to be checked, the electricity is turned off well in advance.

Where it comes from
A power station makes enough electricity for thousands of homes.

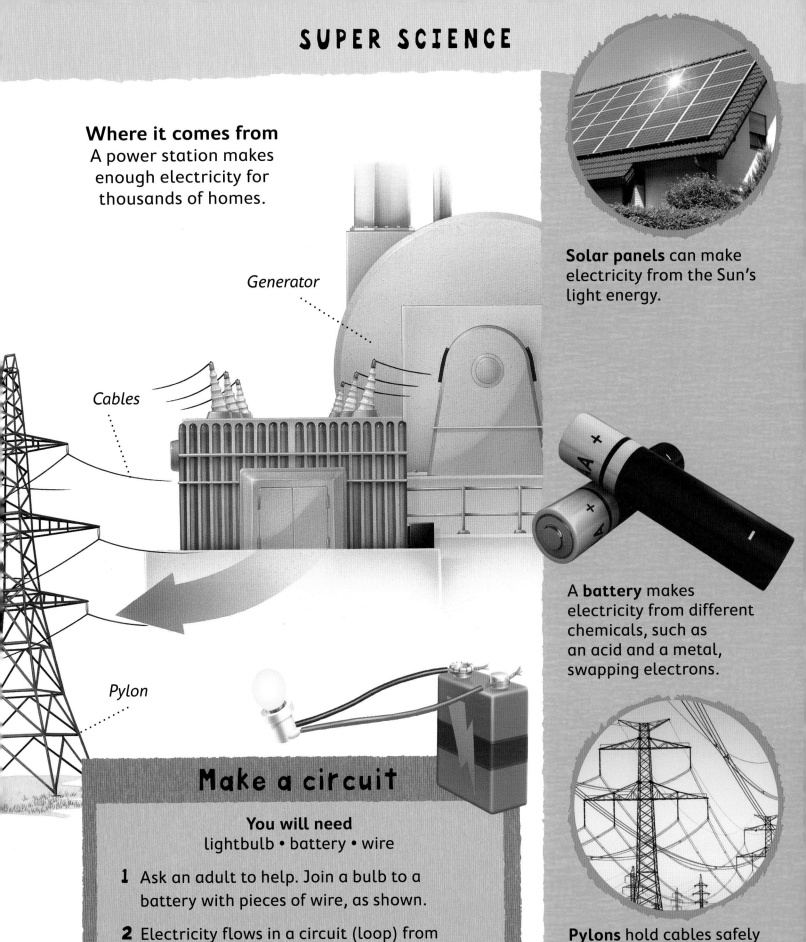

Generator

Cables

Pylon

Solar panels can make electricity from the Sun's light energy.

A **battery** makes electricity from different chemicals, such as an acid and a metal, swapping electrons.

Pylons hold cables safely above the ground.

Make a circuit

You will need
lightbulb • battery • wire

1 Ask an adult to help. Join a bulb to a battery with pieces of wire, as shown.

2 Electricity flows in a circuit (loop) from the battery and through the wires to the lightbulb, and lights the bulb.

Making sounds and pictures

The air is full of waves we cannot see or hear, unless we have the right machine. Radio waves are a form of electrical and magnetic energy, just like light waves and microwaves. They all travel at an equal speed — the speed of light.

A radio picks up radio waves using its long aerial or antenna and converts them to sound waves

Sometimes radio waves may be sent by a satellite in space

Radio waves

Travelling waves

Radio waves are used for both radio and television. They travel long distances from a satellite to your home, car or workplace.

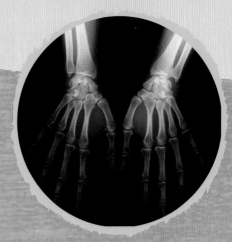

X-rays can go through the soft parts of your body and take pictures of the bones.

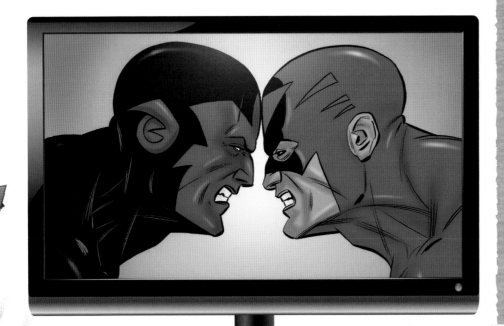

Receiving waves

A radio receiver converts radio waves into sounds. A television receiver or TV set changes them to pictures and sounds.

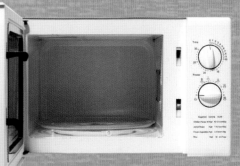

A microwave uses a kind of radio wave (also called a **microwave**) to heat food.

FUN FACT!

Radio waves travel easily though space, but they hardly pass at all through water.

A satellite dish on the outside of a house picks up radio waves for TV channels

Computer science

Computers are amazing machines. We give them instructions and information in various ways. These include typing on a keyboard, inserting a disc, using a joystick, or linking up a camera, scanner or another computer.

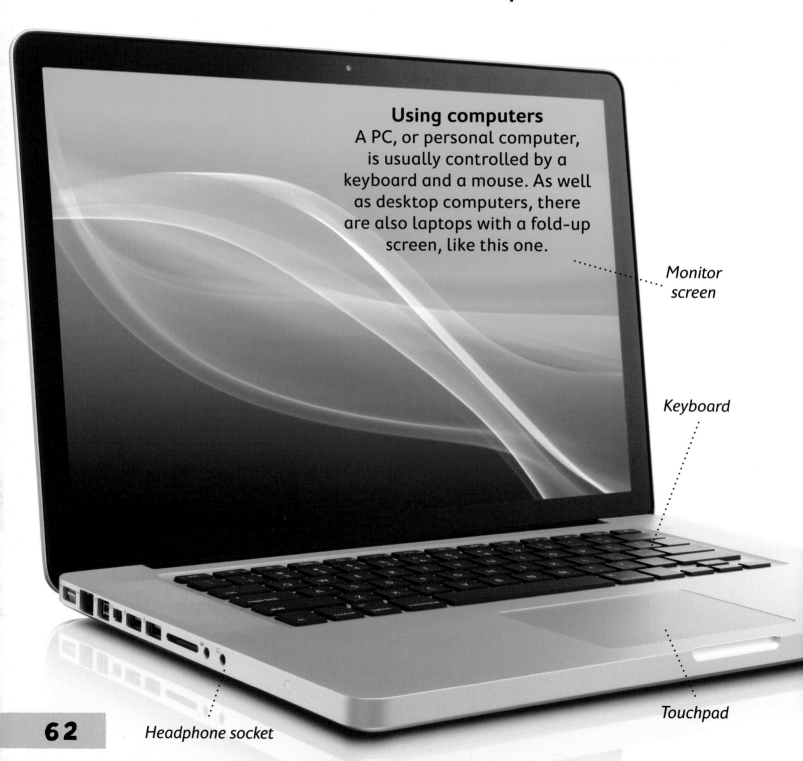

Using computers
A PC, or personal computer, is usually controlled by a keyboard and a mouse. As well as desktop computers, there are also laptops with a fold-up screen, like this one.

Monitor screen

Keyboard

Touchpad

Headphone socket

Microchips are the main 'brain' of a computer.

On a tablet
The iPad was first introduced by Apple in 2010. It is a 'tablet', which works like a computer but is much thinner and lighter.

The **mouse** moves a cursor (pointer) around the computer screen.

Amazing web

The world is at your fingertips if you are on the Internet — a worldwide network of linked computers. Computers, tablets and mobile phones can be used to access it, allowing users to browse web pages, send emails and watch videos.

Information can be stored on a chip inside a **memory stick**.

What is it made of?

You would not make a bridge out of straw, or a cup out of thin paper. Choosing the right material is important. Cars are made from tough, long-lasting materials. Metal, plastic and rubber are all materials used to make cars.

The right substances
A racing car has thousands of parts made from hundreds of materials. Many parts need to be strong, but not weigh much, so the car can go as fast as possible.

The engine is very powerful, but also needs to be light

The main body of the car is made from carbon fibre. It is strong and light, and protects the car from damage

Not built to last

In 2007, this bridge in Minneapolis, USA, collapsed. The road and the vehicles that travelled on it were too heavy.

Plastics are mainly made from oil.

Ceramics are made from clay that is dug from the earth.

Made by nature

Many materials come from plants. Wood comes from the trunks and branches of trees. Cotton comes from the seeds of cotton plants to make clothes such as T-shirts.

Glass is made from limestone and sand.

Mini science

Everything in the world is made of atoms. Atoms are the smallest bits of a substance. They are so tiny that even a billion atoms would be too small to see.

Looking inside

Inside an atom are even smaller bits called subatomic particles. There are three main kinds — protons, neutrons and electrons.

Inside an atom

1. The centre of the atom is called the nucleus. It contains protons (red), and neutrons (black)

2. Around the centre of each atom are subatomic particles called electrons. They whizz round the nucleus.

3. On this illustration, paths indicate the movement of electrons around the nucleus.

Hydrogen is a gas with just one proton.

Proton

Electron

Proton

Neutron

Helium is a gas with two protons and two neutrons.

Proton

Neutron

Oxygen, the gas we need to breathe, has eight protons and eight neutrons.

1

2

3

FUN FACT!

Atoms are so small that a grain of sand contains at least 100 billion billion atoms!

Early dinosaurs

Dinosaurs were a group of scaly-skinned reptiles that lived and died out millions of years ago. The first dinosaurs lived almost **230 million years ago**, in what is now Argentina in South America.

On two legs

Herrerasaurus was a meat-eating dinosaur. It could stand almost upright and run on its two rear legs, making it one of the fastest dinosaurs of its time.

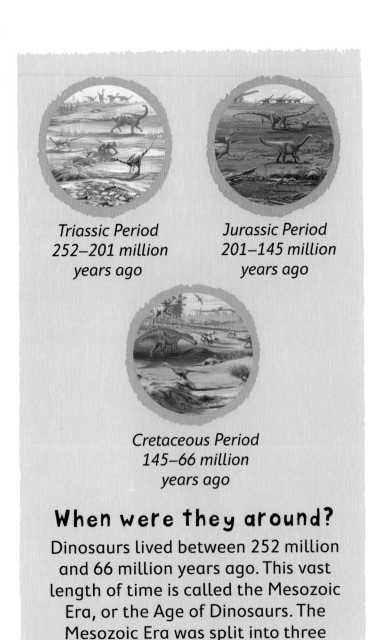

Triassic Period
252–201 million
years ago

Jurassic Period
201–145 million
years ago

Cretaceous Period
145–66 million
years ago

When were they around?

Dinosaurs lived between 252 million and 66 million years ago. This vast length of time is called the Mesozoic Era, or the Age of Dinosaurs. The Mesozoic Era was split into three time periods — the Triassic, Jurassic and Cretaceous.

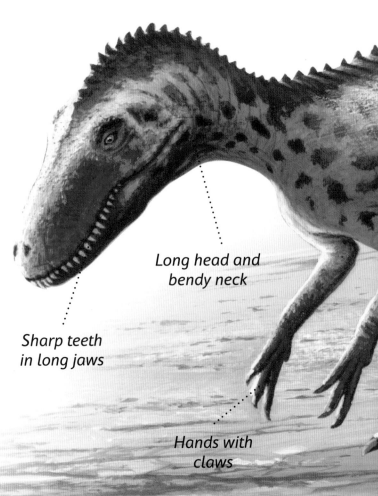

Long head and
bendy neck

Sharp teeth
in long jaws

Hands with
claws

Fewer fingers

Only very few remains of *Saltopus* have been discovered, near Elgin in Scotland. It was a tiny dinosaur, about the size of a small pet cat. The hands of *Saltopus* had five fingers each, which was a primitive (early) feature for a meat-eating dinosaur. Over millions of years the number of fingers reduced to three or even two per hand.

All dinosaurs moved on **land**. They could not fly or live in water.

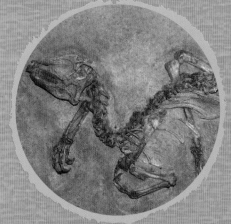

We can learn about dinosaurs through their remains, or **fossils**.

Long tail to keep balance

Long, strong legs

Some **dinosaurs** were plant eaters, while others ate meat.

Gentle giants

Sauropods were dinosaur giants. These enormous creatures all had small heads, long necks, long tails, barrel-shaped bodies and four legs.

Towering above
Barosaurus was one of the biggest sauropods at about 25 metres long. Like most sauropods, *Barosaurus* had to eat for most of the day to get enough goodness for its enormous body.

Size and scale

Some of the biggest sauropods were *Brachiosaurus*, *Argentinosaurus* and *Apatosaurus*. This scale shows how big they were compared to an adult human.

Apatosaurus *was 23 metres long. Its tail had 82 bones and was used to whip enemies*

Brachiosaurus *was 25 metres long. With its long front legs and neck, it could reach food 14 metres from the ground*

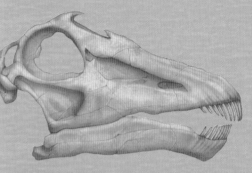

Diplodocus had peg-like teeth for raking up leaves.

Colossal creature

Argentinosaurus was the biggest sauropod at 40 metres in length and 100 tonnes in weight.

Sauropods had claws that were almost flat. Some even looked like they had toenails!

Huge hunters

The biggest meat-eating dinosaurs were the largest hunters ever to have lived. Different types came and went during the Age of Dinosaurs. One of the last dinosaurs was also one of the largest hunters – *Tyrannosaurus rex*.

Massive head measuring 1.6 metres in length

Small, useless arms

Huge feet and powerful legs

Bone-cruncher
Tyrannosaurus rex had sharp teeth up to 25 centimetres in length. Its jaws could crunch through bone.

Built for hunting

Predators like *Tyrannosaurus rex* had strong legs for running, and enormous toe claws for kicking and holding down victims.

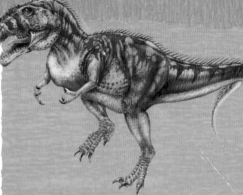

Giganotosaurus had three clawed fingers on each hand.

Spinosaurus is the biggest meat-eating animal that has ever lived.

Powerful predator

Allosaurus was a big, fast-moving hunter with powerful jaws. It lived millions of years before *Tyrannosaurus rex*.

Eyebrow horns

Long tail

Powerful jaws with long teeth

Sharp-clawed hands

Long, strong legs and clawed feet

FUN FACT!

Some meat-eating dinosaurs not only bit their prey, but also each other! Fossils of several tyrannosaurs had bite marks on their heads.

Super senses

Like the reptiles of today, dinosaurs could see, hear and smell the world around them. We know this from the fossils of dead dinosaurs. Fossil skulls have spaces for eyes, ears and nostrils.

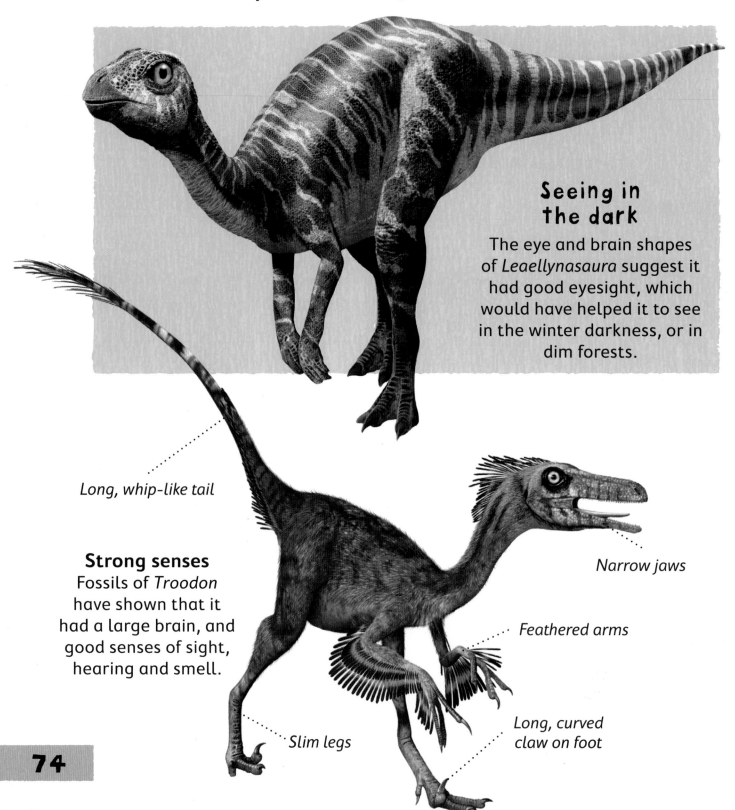

Seeing in the dark

The eye and brain shapes of *Leaellynasaura* suggest it had good eyesight, which would have helped it to see in the winter darkness, or in dim forests.

Long, whip-like tail

Strong senses
Fossils of *Troodon* have shown that it had a large brain, and good senses of sight, hearing and smell.

Narrow jaws

Feathered arms

Slim legs

Long, curved claw on foot

Make a Troodon mask

You will need
card • pencil • paints • paintbrush
scissors • cotton

1 Draw and paint the mask shown here.

2 Carefully cut out the mask and give it two large eye holes.

3 Make a small hole on either side of the mask to thread the cotton through. Tie the mask onto your head to become a *Troodon* dinosaur!

Troodon's skull had large holes for the eye area.

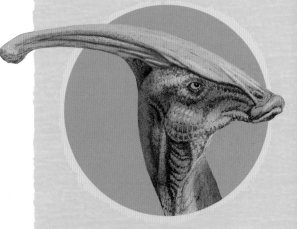

Parasaurolophus may have used the tube-like crest on its head to make a noise like a trumpet.

Brainbox

Tyrannosaurus rex had the biggest brain of almost any dinosaur. Some fossils show the space where its brain would have been, and its shape.

Brain

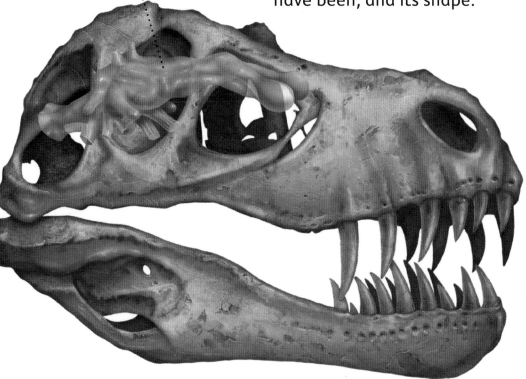

Corythosaurus had a bony plate on its head, instead of a tube.

Slow or speedy?

Dinosaurs moved at different speeds, depending on their size and shape. Today, fast-moving cheetahs and ostriches are slim animals with long legs. Elephants and hippos are heavy and move slowly. Dinosaurs were similar — some were fast and some were slow.

Fast features
Ornithomimus had long, strong legs. It was able to run fast to escape from predators. *Ornithomimus* could reach a speed of 70 kilometres an hour. That's faster than a horse at full gallop!

Feeding time

Ornithomimus' mouth was shaped like a bird's beak. It pecked at all kinds of food such as seeds, worms and bugs. Its head was too small to be able to hunt large prey.

Struthiomimus could run at 80 kilometres an hour.

Coelophysis could run quickly after its prey of lizards and insects.

Make a dinosaur

You will need
pencil • stiff card • paints • paintbrush
scissors • split pins

1 Draw a dinosaur without legs. Paint it any colour you wish and cut it out.

2 Draw two legs on another piece of card. Paint and cut them out, too.

3 Fix the legs on either side of the hip area of the body using a split pin. Now make your dinosaur move!

Muttaburrasaurus could only run at 15 kilometres an hour.

Baby dinosaurs

Like most reptiles today, dinosaurs laid eggs. Fossils of their eggs and of newly hatched babies have been found. Some dinosaurs may have looked after their babies, bringing them food. Fossil finds of *Maiasaura* include nests, eggs, newly hatched young and broken eggshells.

The nest was a mound of mud about 2 metres across and contained about 20 eggs

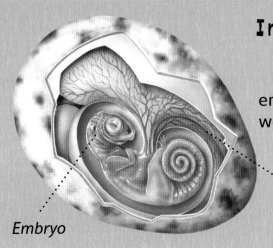

Inside the egg

A baby dinosaur developed as an embryo in its egg. It was fed by nutrients from the yolk.

Yolk

Embryo

Some dinosaurs laid **eggs** that were 50 times as big as a hen's egg.

Hungry babies

Newly hatched *Maiasaura* babies stayed in their nest until their legs were strong enough for them to move around. The parents brought food to the nest for the babies to eat.

Some babies hatched by **biting** through the tough shell.

FUN FACT!

Baby dinosaurs grew up to five times faster than human babies. Some were already one metre long when they hatched!

Baby Maiasaura were only 30 to 40 centimetres long

Dinosaurs in battle

Some dinosaurs had body defences, such as spikes, to protect them from predators. Most armoured dinosaurs were plant eaters. They had to defend themselves against meat eaters such as *Tyrannosaurus rex*.

Spinosaurus *was a deadly carnivore with large, sharp teeth*

Armour and weapons
Ankylosaurus could defend itself well. It had a large tail club to hit predators, and its head and back were protected by large bony lumps and plates.

Design a dinosaur

You will need
pencil • paper • paints • paintbrush

1 Draw your own dinosaur – you could add horns, sharp teeth, sharp claws, a long tail, big eyes – anything you want!

2 No one knows what colour dinosaurs actually were, so you could paint your dinosaur any colour – purple and green with red spikes!

3 Name your dinosaur. You could name it after yourself, like *Clarosaurus* or *Pauloceratops*!

Triceratops had three horns, one on its nose and two above its eyes.

Edmontonia had bony lumps on its head, back and tail, and rows of spikes along its neck and sides.

Euoplocephalus had pointed lumps of bone across its back.

Ankylosaurus' tail club was one metre across and could deliver a painful blow

Ankylosaurus had spikes and lumps of bone on its back to protect itself

Where did they go?

The dinosaurs died out 65 million years ago. There are dinosaur fossils in rocks up to this time, but none after this. However, there are fossils of creatures such as fish and mammals. Perhaps a giant rock (meteorite) from space smashed into Earth, killing the dinosaurs.

Deadly meteorite
A meteorite would have thrown up clouds of ash and dust, blocking out the Sun. Plants would have died, leaving no food for the plant-eating dinosaurs. When the plant eaters died, the meat-eating dinosaurs would have starved.

Erupting volcanoes

Volcanoes around Earth could have erupted at the same time. This would have thrown out red-hot rocks, ash, dust and clouds of poison gas. Dinosaurs would have choked and died in the gloom.

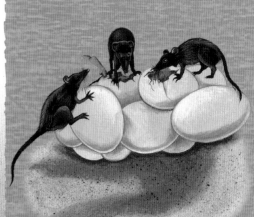

Other animals may have eaten all the dinosaur eggs.

A **giant wave** may have drowned the dinosaurs.

Ocean mammals

Many animals that live in the sea, such as whales and dolphins, are warm-blooded mammals. They need to come to the surface to breathe air. Dolphins can only hold their breath for a few minutes, but sperm whales can hold their breath for up to two hours.

Working together
Bottlenose dolphins swim together around a group of fish. By working as a team, they can catch more fish to eat.

Keeping warm
Polar bears live at the North Pole. They are good swimmers — thick fur and a layer of fat under their skin keeps them warm in the icy sea.

Most **seals** live in cold waters in the Arctic and Antarctic.

Dugongs feed on sea grass and algae on the seabed.

FUN FACT!

Barnacles are shellfish. They attach themselves to ships' hulls, or the bodies of grey whales and other large sea animals.

Ocean reptiles

Cold-blooded creatures, such as reptiles, cannot control their body temperature. Most of them prefer to live on land, where it is easier for them to warm up. Some reptiles have adapted to ocean life, such as marine iguanas.

Sunbathing on the rocks
When marine iguanas are not diving for food, they bask in the sunshine around the coastline. The lizards' dark skin helps them to absorb (take in) the Sun's heat.

Sneaky snake
The yellow-bellied sea snake has a sneaky trick. Once its bright underside has attracted a fish, it darts backwards — so the fish is next to its open mouth, ready to be eaten.

The diet of the beautiful **hawksbill turtle** consists mainly of sea sponges.

Looking for food
Banded sea snakes swim around coral reefs in search of their favourite food — eels.

Adult **green turtles** feed mostly on plants such as sea grasses and algae.

Super saltie
Crocodiles mainly live in wetlands, rivers and lakes, but the saltwater crocodile can live in saltwater or freshwater.

Turtles lay eggs on land. Once hatched, the **babies** must make their own way down to the water.

Deep-sea creatures

Few creatures can survive in the dark, icy-cold ocean depths. Food is so hard to find that some animals have unusual features, such as invisible teeth and their own fishing rods, to help them survive.

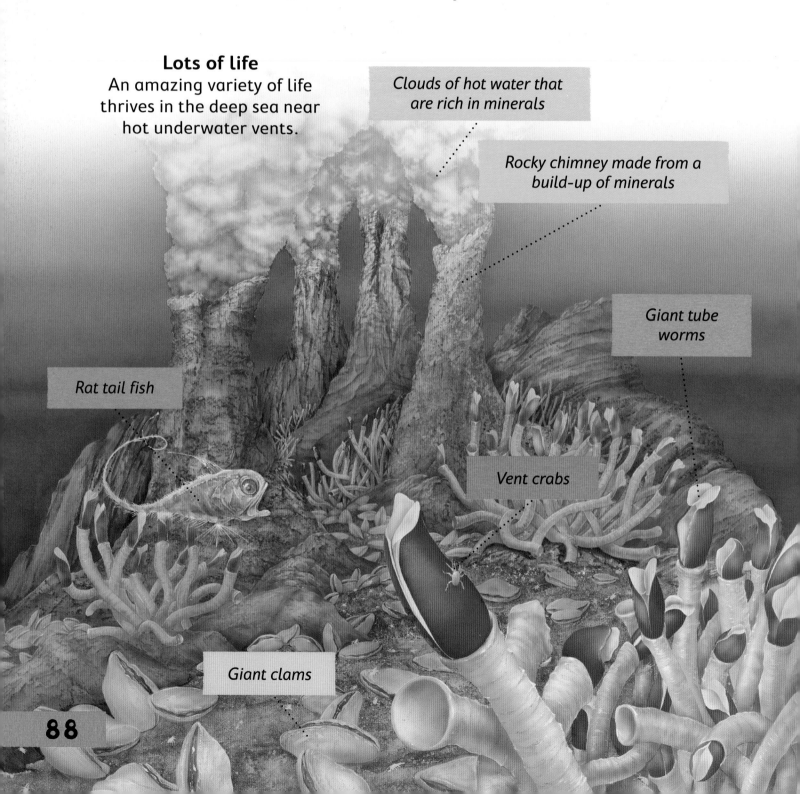

Lots of life
An amazing variety of life thrives in the deep sea near hot underwater vents.

Clouds of hot water that are rich in minerals

Rocky chimney made from a build-up of minerals

Giant tube worms

Rat tail fish

Vent crabs

Giant clams

A **barreleye fish's** eyes are very sensitive, which helps it to spot its prey.

Monster of the deep
Giant squid grow up to 15 metres in length. They have long, powerful tentacles and huge eyes.

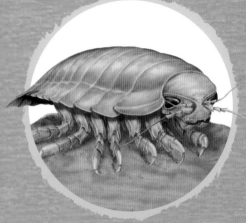

Giant isopods have long antennae, so they can feel their way in the dark.

In the dark
Fangtooth fish don't have good eyesight. Instead they can sense tiny movements in the water made by their prey.

Gulper eels have enormous mouths for scooping up lots of prey in one mouthful.

Super swimmers

There are more than 21,000 different types of fish. Almost all of them are covered in scales and use fins and a muscular tail to power themselves through the water. They have slits called gills that take oxygen from the water so that they can breathe.

Ocean schools
A large group of fish is called a school or shoal. The fish are protected from hunters when there are such large numbers.

Hidden on the seabed
The shape and colour of flounders help to camouflage them on the seabed.

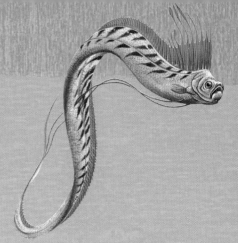

Strong sharks

Sharks are meat eaters. Some filter tiny prey from the water, or lie in wait for victims on the seabed. Others speed through the ocean after prey.

Oarfish grow up to 8 metres long. Their length helps to protect them from hunters.

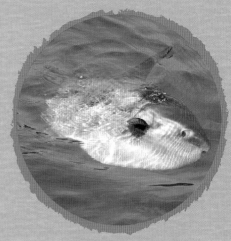

Sunfish were given their name because they like to sunbathe at the ocean surface.

FUN FACT!

Flying fish can use their wing-like fins to keep them in the air for as long as 30 seconds!

Fast flippers

Seals, sea lions and walruses are warm-blooded mammals that have adapted to ocean life. They have flippers instead of legs and a streamlined body. Instead of fur, they have a layer of fat called blubber to keep them warm in cold waters.

Super swimmers

Leopard seals spend most of their lives in water and attack penguins when they swim and dive. They have long, sharp teeth to bite into the flesh of their prey.

Giant of the ocean
The male southern elephant seal is as big as a real elephant. It is almost 6 metres long and weighs about 5 tonnes.

Sea otters live around the Pacific coast among huge forests of seaweed.

Walruses use their tusks to break breathing holes in the ice.

Making noise
Sea lions get their name because they make a loud roaring sound. Unlike seals, they have ear flaps on their heads.

FUN FACT!
Leopard seals are noisy! They chirp and whistle in their sleep.

Great travellers

Many ocean animals migrate (travel) incredible distances every year. They have different reasons for doing this. Some travel to certain places for breeding. Others migrate south in the winter to reach warmer climates.

On the move
Loggerhead turtles are born on beaches in Japan. As soon as they have hatched from their eggs, they hurry to the sea and make a two-year journey to Mexico. They return to Japan to breed.

Round trip
Arctic terns can fly more than 40,000 kilometres in one year. They travel from breeding areas in the Arctic to the Antarctic, and back again, each year.

Salmon live in the ocean. They travel into rivers to lay their eggs.

Long journey
During the summer, humpback whales migrate to the icy waters in the north and south of the world. In winter, they breed in tropical waters.

Spiny lobsters travel in long columns by touch, using their long, spiky antennae (feelers).

What are mammals?

There are thousands of mammals living on Earth. Some can swim, some can fly and all are warm-blooded. Being warm-blooded means that mammals can keep their body temperature the same in any weather conditions.

In the ocean
There are more than 35 different kinds of dolphin. The dusky dolphin likes to swim near boats, and can leap and somersault above the waves.

FUN FACT!

Dolphins can travel and feed in groups of up to 2000!

FANTASTIC MAMMALS

Pangolins are covered in hard scales for protection.

Red pandas sleep during the day and feed at night.

Motherly love
Orang-utans are the largest mammals to live in trees. Like all mammals, young orang-utans feed on their mother's milk.

Elephants on parade

You will need
paper • pens • scissors

1 Fold a long sheet of paper backwards and forwards into wide zigzags.

2 Draw an elephant shape onto the top page, with the tail joined to one edge and the trunk to the other.

3 Cut around the outline.

4 Draw ears and eyes onto each shape and colour them in. Open out your chain. All the elephants are holding trunks and tails!

Beavers have flat tails and webbed feet, making them excellent swimmers.

Baby mammals

Most mammals give birth to their babies but some, such as the duck-billed platypus, lay eggs. All baby mammals drink their mother's milk. It contains all the goodness they need to grow.

Spotty cubs
The female puma, or mountain lion, gives birth to cubs with spotted fur. The spots disappear as the cubs grow older.

FANTASTIC MAMMALS

A troop of chimps

A pack of wolves

A harem of seals

Mammal families

Some mammals live alone, except for when they have young. Other mammals like to live in groups. There are different names for these groups, depending on the animal.

Elephants have the **longest pregnancies** of any mammal — about 20 months.

Lots of babies

Virginia opossums have more babies than any other mammal — as many as 21.

A **baby gorilla** may stay with its mother for up to four years.

River mammals

Most river mammals spend only part of their time in water. Creatures such as the river otter and the water rat live on land and go into the water to find food. The hippopotamus, however, spends most of its day in water to keep cool.

Strong swimmer
Webbed feet help to push the water vole through the water.

Living in water
The water opossum dives into rivers to find fish. It has waterproof fur and webbed back feet.

Mammal mix-up

You will need
pens • paper • friends

1 The first player draws the head of a mammal, giving it a long neck, then folds over the paper, so that only the neck shows, and passes it on.

2 Without looking under the fold, the next player adds a body to the neck, and folds the paper again.

3 The third player draws legs and feet and passes it to the last player. Unfold the paper. What a mix-up!

In the depths
The platypus uses its duck-like beak to find food in the murky riverbed. It has webbed feet to help it swim through the water.

Manatees are water-living mammals that feed on plants.

Hippos are not good swimmers. Instead, they walk on the riverbed.

Snow mammals

Mammals that live in very cold places, such as the Arctic and Antarctic, have thick fur to keep them warm. The colour of their fur is very important as it helps them to hide in the snow.

Arctic hunter
The polar bear is the biggest land mammal in the Arctic. It can run fast, swim well and even dive under the ice to hunt its main prey – seals.

FUN FACT!

The polar bear needs its thick fur to keep out the Arctic cold – even the soles of its feet are furry!

Big paws
The snow leopard lives in the mountains of central Asia. It has large paws to help it walk on the snow.

Male walruses have long teeth called tusks, for digging up shellfish from the seabed.

Musk oxen have long shaggy coats to help them to survive the Arctic cold.

Waterproof fur
Harp seals are surrounded by snow, ice and freezing cold water. The adults' thick fur is waterproof so they can dive into the sea to catch fish.

Snowshoe hares have brown coats in summer, which then turn white in winter.

103

Fins and flippers

Most swimming mammals have flippers and fins instead of legs. Seals and sea lions have paddle-like flippers. They use them to drag themselves along on land, as well as for swimming. Whales and dolphins never come onto land. They use their tails and flippers to swim.

Smooth swimmers

Many kinds of dolphin live in groups called schools. They have smooth skin to help them slip easily through the water.

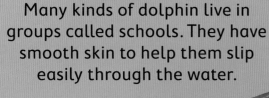

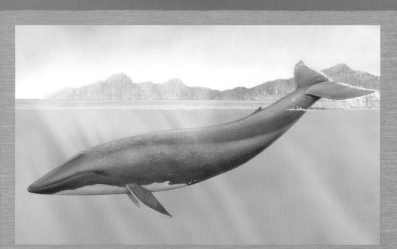

Record-breaker

The blue whale is the biggest mammal — and the biggest animal ever to have lived on Earth. It can reach 33.5 metres in length — as long as seven family cars parked end to end.

FANTASTIC MAMMALS

The **grey whale** dives to the seafloor to feed using filters in its mouth called baleen.

Dolphins are energetic, and can often be seen leaping from the water.

Flipper

Amazing acrobatics

Humpback whales can weigh up to 30 tonnes, but they are able to leap out of the water using their powerful flippers and tail.

Killer whales are the largest members of the dolphin family.

In the rainforest

Rainforest mammals live at all levels of the forest, from the tallest trees to the forest floor. Bats fly over the tree tops and monkeys and apes swing from branch to branch. Lower down, smaller creatures, such as civets and pottos, hide among the thick greenery.

Down in the swamp
Jaguars live in the rainforests of Central and South America. They are strong swimmers, and can often be found in swampy areas.

FANTASTIC MAMMALS

Tops of the trees
The aye-aye is related to the lemur. It has an unusually long middle finger, so it can dig into trees and pull out grubs to eat.

Tapirs live on the rainforest floor and have long, bendy snouts.

Agoutis have strong teeth that can bite through hard nut shells.

Moving around
Ring-tailed lemurs only live on the island of Madagascar. In the rainforest, they walk along the ground and move through the trees.

FUN FACT!
The sloth spends so much time upside down that its fur grows downwards – the opposite way to most mammals. This is so rainwater drips off more easily.

Desert life

Mammals that live in the desert have developed ways to escape the scorching heat. The North African gerbil burrows underground and only comes out at night. Not all deserts are hot — the Gobi Desert in Asia can be cold during winter.

Keeping warm
The camel has thick fur to keep it warm during the Gobi Desert's cold winter.

108

FANTASTIC MAMMALS

The **desert kangaroo rat** comes out at night to find seeds.

Finding water
Wildebeest find areas where there is enough water to drink.

Hyenas are good hunters, and sometimes steal other animals' food.

No water wasted
Desert-dwelling scorpions and reptiles have watertight body coverings, which lose little water.

Fennec foxes have large ears to help them lose heat.

Plant food

Plant eaters spend much of their time eating in order to get enough nourishment (goodness from food). The good side to being a plant eater is that the animal does not have to chase and fight for its food as hunters do.

Panda's plant
Nearly all of the panda's diet is bamboo. It eats fresh shoots in spring, mature leaves in summer and stems in winter.

Long tongue

The giraffe's black tongue is almost 30 centimetres long. It uses it to grip leaves and pull them into its mouth.

Munching lemurs

Lemurs mainly eat plants. They live in tropical forests where there are lots of fresh leaves and ripe fruit all year round.

Rabbits have strong teeth for eating leaves and bark.

Rhinos can be heard munching on plants from 400 metres away.

Wombats feed on the grass around their burrow.

111

Hungry hunters

Mammals that hunt and kill other creatures are called carnivores. Lions, tigers, wolves and dogs are all carnivores. Many carnivores do not have to hunt every day – one kill will last them for several days.

Meat and plants
Bears are carnivores, but many eat more plants than meat. In summer, brown bears wade into rivers and catch fish.

Wolves hunt in packs, so they can kill larger animals.

Practice makes perfect

The tiger is an expert hunter. Creeping up on its prey, such as deer, it pounces and kills its victim quickly.

A pack of **hunting dogs** will try to separate one animal from the rest of its herd.

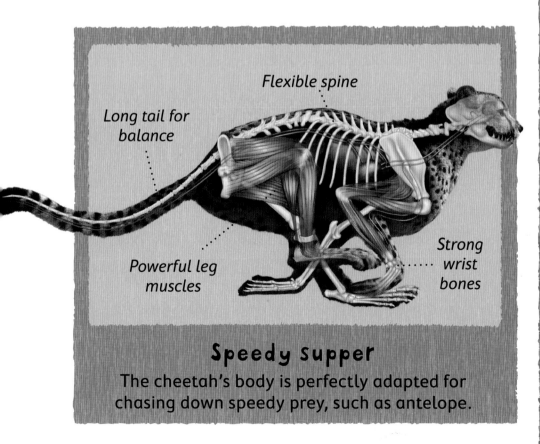

Flexible spine

Long tail for balance

Powerful leg muscles

Strong wrist bones

Speedy Supper

The cheetah's body is perfectly adapted for chasing down speedy prey, such as antelope.

Caracals can leap 3 metres into the air to catch a passing bird.

What is a bird?

All birds have two legs, a pair of wings and a body that is covered in feathers. There are more than 9000 different species (types) of bird, and they live all over the world, from icy Antarctica to the hottest deserts.

Safe and sound

All birds lay eggs with a hard shell. This protects the growing young. The parent birds keep the eggs safe and warm until the chicks hatch.

New life

Once the chicks (baby birds) hatch from their eggs, they need to be fed regularly to help them grow stronger.

114

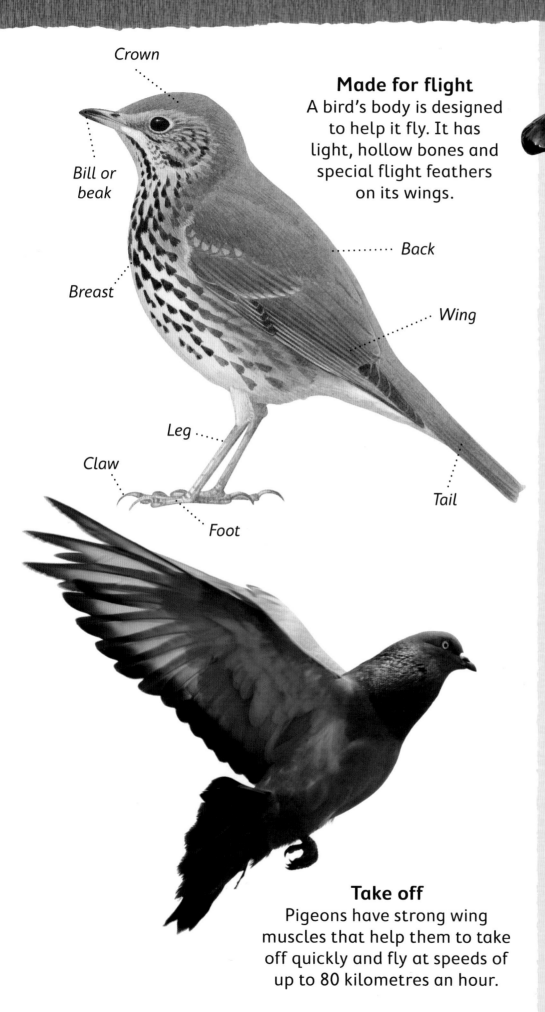

Crown

Bill or beak

Breast

Made for flight
A bird's body is designed to help it fly. It has light, hollow bones and special flight feathers on its wings.

Back

Wing

Leg

Claw

Tail

Foot

Take off
Pigeons have strong wing muscles that help them to take off quickly and fly at speeds of up to 80 kilometres an hour.

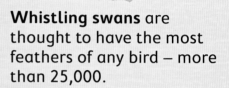

Whistling swans are thought to have the most feathers of any bird – more than 25,000.

Ostriches have strong legs so they can run fast.

Hornbills have horn-like growths on their beaks called casques.

Starting life

A bird's egg protects the chick growing inside. The yolk provides food, while layers of egg white cushion the chick. The shell is hard but porous - it allows air in and out. Once hatched, the young of some species are reared (brought up) by their parents. Others find their own food as soon as they hatch.

Time to hatch
When it is ready to hatch, the chick chips away at the egg shell and breaks free.

1 *The chick starts to crack the egg*

Escape tools
An egg tooth is a small, sharp lump on a chick's beak that helps it to break the eggshell when it is time to hatch.

2 *The chick uses its egg tooth to break the shell*

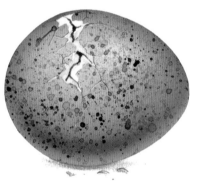

3 *The egg splits wide open*

4 *The chick is able to wriggle free. Its parents will look after it for several weeks until it can care for itself*

116

Ducklings follow the first moving thing they see when they hatch — usually their mother.

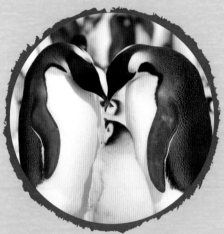

Emperor penguins only lay a single egg each year. Rearing a chick in such a harsh environment is very difficult.

On a cliff
Guillemots live on cliff tops. They do not build nests, but simply lay their eggs on the rock or bare earth.

Keeping eggs warm
Parent birds, such as the emu, take turns to sit on the eggs to keep them warm. This is called incubation.

FUN FACT!

The guillemot's egg is pear-shaped, so that if the egg is pushed or knocked, it does not roll off the cliff.

Bird homes

Birds make nests in which to lay their eggs and keep them safe. Nests can be made of twigs, leaves, mud or saliva. They are built in a variety of places, such as trees, near water or in the walls of buildings.

The biggest nest
The bald eagle makes one of the biggest nests of any bird. It is made of sticks and built in a tree or on rocks.

118

Hanging home

The male weaver bird makes a nest from grass and stems. He knots and weaves the pieces together to make a long nest, which hangs from the branch of a tree.

1 *The male weaver bird twists strips of leaves around a branch or twig*

2 *Then, he makes a roof and an entrance*

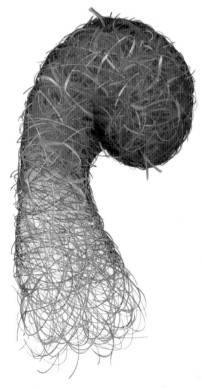

3 *When the nest is finished, the long entrance helps to provide a safe shelter for the eggs*

Swallows often make their nests in the eaves of buildings, near the roof.

Cuckoos don't make their own nests. Instead, they lay eggs in other birds' nests.

FUN FACT!

Sometimes people collect the nests of cave swiftlets to make bird's nest soup!

Swimmers and divers

Penguins are the best swimmers and divers in the bird world. They spend most of their lives in water, using their wings as strong flippers to help them swim.

Long dives
Emperor penguins can dive for more than 18 minutes. Their tail and webbed feet help them steer through the water.

All kinds of penguin
There are 17 different types of penguin, mainly living in the Antarctic. They form large groups called rookeries, especially at breeding time.

Short dives
Arctic terns catch fish and other creatures by making short dives into the water.

Northern gannets dive from great heights to catch fish from the sea.

Upside down
Some types of duck find food by turning themselves upside down to search under the surface of the water — this is called dabbling.

Eagles are very skilled at plucking fish from the water.

121

Feeding time

All birds have a beak for eating. They have different kinds of beak, suited to the types of food they eat. Insect-eating birds have thin, sharp beaks for picking up tiny prey. Hunting birds have hooked beaks for tearing flesh.

Eating insects

The European bee-eater uses its sharp beak to catch bees, wasps and dragonflies. Once it has snapped up an insect, it rubs its catch on a branch to get rid of the sting.

Eggs for dinner

The Egyptian vulture steals other birds' eggs. It cracks the eggs by dropping them on the ground or by dropping stones on them.

Hummingbirds use their long tongues to sip the nectar inside flowers.

A nutty treat
Nuthatches feed on nuts and seeds as well as some insects. They have a long pointed beak and can hang upside down so they can easily get at food.

Vultures have bald heads so they don't get messy when eating dead animals.

Fish food
Puffins have large colourful beaks, which can hold 12 or more fish. This is very useful, as puffins fill their beaks and carry the food back to their young.

Oxpeckers pull ticks from the skin of animals such as antelopes.

Fierce hunters

Eagles, hawks and owls are all birds of prey – birds that hunt other animals. The golden eagle is one of the fiercest birds of prey. When it spies a victim, the golden eagle dives down and seizes the prey in its powerful claws, called talons.

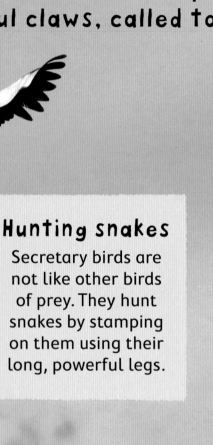

Hunting snakes

Secretary birds are not like other birds of prey. They hunt snakes by stamping on them using their long, powerful legs.

Food on the wing

Philippine eagles hunt from perches. They eat lots of different animals, such as flying lemurs, monkeys, bats and snakes. Philippine eagles are very rare, and are protected by law.

Bald eagles will eat almost anything, from carrion to fish.

Ravens mainly hunt rats and mice, but they can catch larger animals, such as rabbits.

Use your feet!

You will need
different sized objects such as pencils, coins and books

1 Get your friends together to see if you can pick things up using your feet – just like an eagle.

2 Start with the easiest object, such as a pencil. Make the objects harder and harder to pick up with your feet. Whoever can pick up the most objects is the winner!

Most **hawks** are useful to humans because they hunt rodents that damage crops.

Rainforest birds

Rainforests are home to a huge variety of bird life — one fifth of all birds live in the Amazon rainforest, in South America. Colourful birds of paradise live in the rainforests of Australia and New Guinea.

Bright colours

The scarlet macaw is named after its bright-red feathers. It lives in the tropical forests of South America, feeding on fruits and seeds.

A rare sight

The blue bird of paradise is very rare and can only be found in New Guinea and north-eastern Australia.

Quetzals' tail feathers grow up to 90 centimetres long.

Toucans all have large, brightly coloured beaks to help attract mates.

Powerful beak
Found in the South American rainforests, the hyacinth macaw has a very powerful beak to crack open hard nuts and seeds.

Rainbow lorikeets feed high up in the rainforest canopy.

Grey parrots
Common in African rainforests, grey parrots feed on fruits and seeds.

Snow birds

The coldest places on Earth are the Arctic and the Antarctic. Here it is too cold for most birds to live all year round. In the Antarctic, most of the land is always covered in ice.

Life on ice
Most penguin species live in the Antarctic. They have a thick layer of fat under their skin to protect them from the cold.

The ptarmigan has white feathers to help it hide from enemies.

Arctic hunting
The snowy owl is the biggest hunting bird of the Arctic region. Snowy owls make their nests on the ground, among stones and moss.

The snow bunting lives and breeds on islands around the Antarctic.

Handy penguins

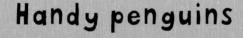

You will need
glue • white cloth • black sock
card • scissors • cotton • buttons

1 Glue the piece of white cloth to the black sock to make chest feathers.

2 Make a beak out of card and attach it to the sock with some cotton. Stick on button eyes.

3 Cut holes in either side and push your hand into the sock, using your fingers as flippers.

The tundra swan brings up its young in the Arctic.

River life

Many birds live near rivers, lakes and marshes.
There are plenty of fish, insects and plants
to eat and places to nest.

Watching the water
The kingfisher perches on a branch
along streams and riverbanks,
watching for any signs of movement
of fish in the water. Then it swoops
down to catch its prey.

Fast dippers
The dipper lives
around fast-flowing
streams and can swim
and dive well.

Wading birds

Storks are wading birds, so they have long, spindly legs and a long beak for plucking fish from the water. Some storks also eat other creatures such as frogs and insects.

Herons stand in shallow water and grab their prey with their sharp beaks.

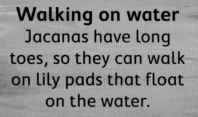

Pelicans collect fish in the big pouch that hangs beneath their long beaks.

Walking on water
Jacanas have long toes, so they can walk on lily pads that float on the water.

Ospreys are found near rivers and lakes. They feed mainly on fish.

What is a bug?

If a creepy-crawly has six legs, it is an insect. If it has more legs or none at all, then it is another kind of animal. The young of some insects have no legs until they become adults.

Common fly
Houseflies are one of the most common insects. They feed on liquid food with sponge-like mouthparts.

Sticky pads and sharp claws help houseflies walk upside down

Tiny ticks
Ticks have eight legs so they are arachnids, not insects. They feed on both animal and human blood.

When ticks start to drink blood, their soft bodies stretch as they swell

Snails are molluscs. They have hard shells to protect their soft bodies.

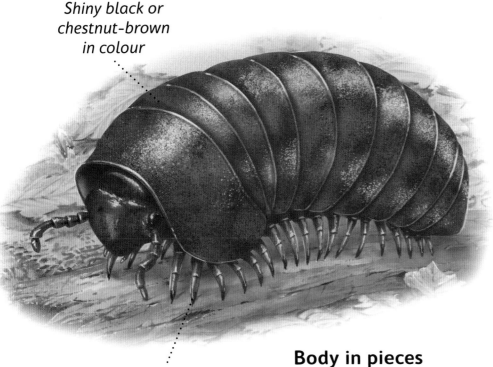

Shiny black or chestnut-brown in colour

About 18 pairs of legs

Body in pieces
Pill millipedes belong to the myriapod animal group. Their bodies have 12 segments.

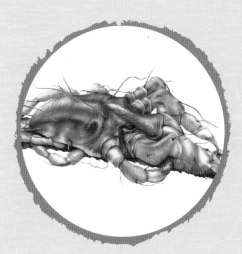

Mites belong to the arachnid family along with spiders and ticks.

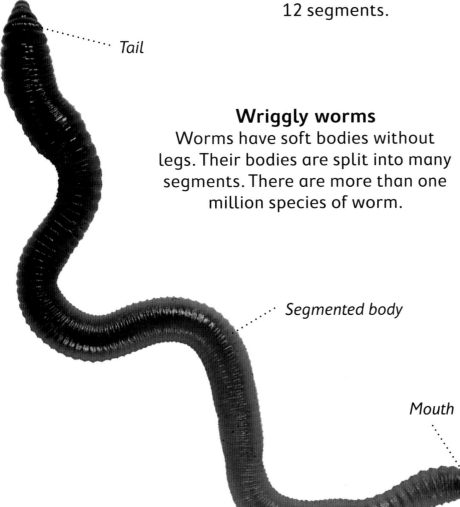

Tail

Wriggly worms
Worms have soft bodies without legs. Their bodies are split into many segments. There are more than one million species of worm.

Segmented body

Mouth

Millipedes have up to 400 pairs of legs and, like centipedes, belong to the myriapod animal group.

The insect world

Insects form the largest of all animal groups, with millions of different kinds, or species. They are found almost everywhere in the world. Common insects include flies, ladybirds, butterflies, ants and bees.

Making honey
Honeybees live in nests called hives. They share jobs such as finding food, cleaning the nest and caring for young.

Some holes in the nest contain honey the bees have made from flower nectar and pollen

A bee's sting is at the end of its body. If it stings an enemy, this part is torn away, and the bee dies

FUN FACT!

As bees collect pollen, they spread it from flower to flower, to make new seeds. If there were fewer bees, there would be fewer flowers.

Cockchafer beetles can be found in woodland, farmland and gardens.

Colourful beetles

Ladybirds have round bodies. They are brightly coloured to put off predators.

Male **scorpionflies** have a harmless sting on a long, curved tail.

A bees' nest has hundreds of six-sided holes with wax walls

Earwigs live in dark, damp corners. They are mostly active at night.

Insect homes

Some insects live together in huge groups called colonies. There are four main types of insect that build large nests — termites, bees, wasps and ants.

Cutting leaves

Leafcutter ants bite off pieces of leaves and carry them to their nest. Here, they chew the leaves into a pile of mush, which rots and grows a type of fungus that the ants like to eat.

AWESOME BUGS

Paper nests
Some wasps build nests of paper, made from chewed-up bits of plants and wood.

Termites make their nests inside huge piles of mud and earth.

Cave crickets like to live in caves and other dark, damp places.

Ants build large, complex nests either on or under the ground.

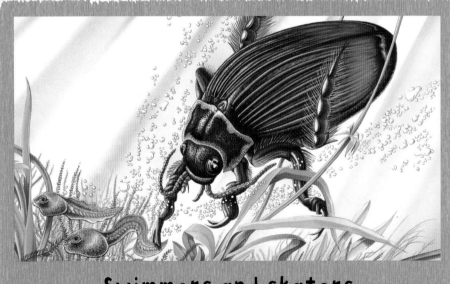

Swimmers and skaters
Many insects live in or near ponds, streams, rivers and lakes. The great diving beetle lives in ponds. It is fast and fierce, with big, sharp jaws to grab and eat animals such as tadpoles.

Taking flight

Many insects can fly. The wings are attached to the middle part of their body, called the thorax. Most insects have two pairs of wings.

The hard outer wings are called elytra. They are red with black spots

The outer wings part to reveal the soft, flying wings underneath

Special wings
Ladybirds fly using their soft inner wings. They fly to look for food, to find new homes and to escape danger.

Up and away!

You will need
stiff card • scissors • sticky tape • tissue paper

1 Carefully fold the stiff card to make a cube-shaped box with two open ends.

2 Attach strips of stiff card to the sides to make struts for the wings. Make the wings from tissue paper and attach to the main box and the struts.

3 Hold the box as shown. Move the top and bottom walls in, then out. This bends the side walls to make the wings flap.

Apollo butterflies are strong fliers. They can fly to the top of mountains.

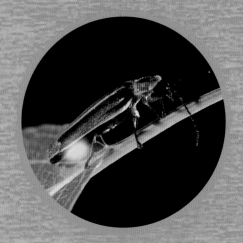

Fireflies are actually beetles. They flash bright lights to attract mates.

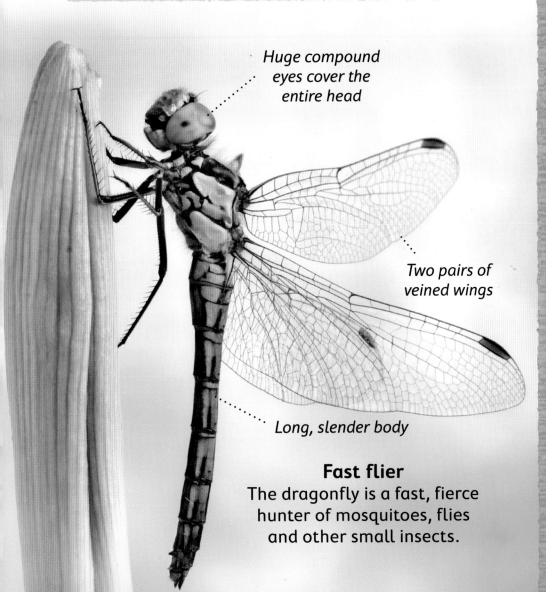

Huge compound eyes cover the entire head

Two pairs of veined wings

Long, slender body

Fast flier
The dragonfly is a fast, fierce hunter of mosquitoes, flies and other small insects.

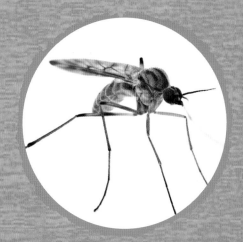

Mosquitoes are small, widespread flies with scaly wings.

Hop, skip and jump

Many insects move around by hopping and jumping, rather than flying. They have long, strong legs and can leap great distances. This helps them to escape from enemies.

Leaping to safety
Grasshoppers have six legs and a pair of large wings. They prefer to escape from danger by leaping rather than flying.

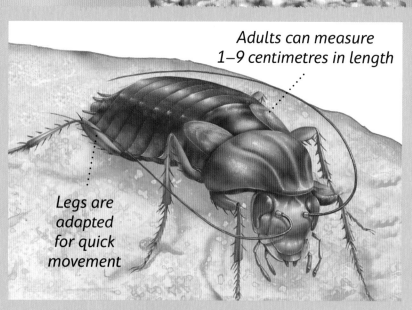

Adults can measure 1–9 centimetres in length

Legs are adapted for quick movement

Speedy bugs
Some insects rarely jump or fly. Instead, they prefer to run. Cockroaches are champion sprinters – they scurry speedily across the ground on long legs.

Long jump
Leafhoppers are strong fliers, but they can also jump great distances.

Crickets are all born with wings, but some cannot fly and only hop from place to place.

Powerful spring
Grasshoppers have very long back legs. Some types can jump more than 3 metres.

Fleas are tiny insects, but they can jump over 30 centimetres in length.

FUN FACT!

Click beetles can flick themselves an amazing 25 centimetres up into the air.

Dinner time

Almost all insects eat plants. They feed on the sap (liquid) in stems and leaves, the nectar in flowers and the soft flesh of fruits and berries. However, some insects are fierce hunters.

Stinky meal
Dung beetles roll animal droppings into big, round balls. They roll the balls into their nests and feed on them.

Furniture beetles like to eat the dead parts of trees and wood.

Nibbling wood
Termites feed on decaying wood, tree stumps and the roots of plants.

Sap feeder
Spittlebugs are also known as froghoppers due to their frog-like appearance. They feed on plant sap.

Death's head hawk-moth caterpillars feed on potato plants and tomato leaves.

Red-banded sand wasps use their strong jaws to pierce their preys' thin skin. Then they inject poison to paralyze the victim.

FUN FACT!
Many insect species eat animal droppings. Some beetles lay their eggs in droppings, then the larvae hatch out and eat the dung!

What is a spider?

Spiders are not insects – they belong to a group called arachnids. All spiders are hunters, using their fangs to grab prey and inject poison. Not all of them use webs – some chase their prey, and others hide until a suitable meal passes by.

Small head

Fangs to inject venom

Large, oval abdomen

Four pairs of legs

Spider anatomy
Spiders usually have eight eyes, eight legs, and are venomous. Their bodies are made up of two parts – the cephalothorax (head and thorax) and the abdomen (body).

Tiny killer
The Australian redback spider belongs to the most deadly group of spiders – the widow spiders.

Sharp fangs
The king baboon tarantula injects venom into small animals, such as mice.

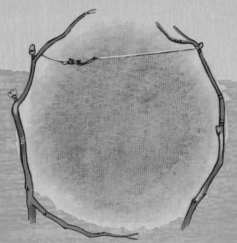

Make a spider's web

You will need
card • scissors • cotton • PVA glue

1 Cut a large, circular hole out of the middle of the card. Stretch a piece of cotton from one edge of the circle to the other, and glue to both sides.

2 Do the same again several times at different angles. Make sure all the threads cross at the centre of the hole.

3 Starting at the centre, glue a long piece of thread to each of the threads. Work your way round in a spiral until you reach the edge. This is how a spider makes a web.

Stage 1
A spider starts a web by building a bridge.

Stage 2
More threads are added to make a strong framework.

Deadly bite
Sydney funnel webs are found in Australia. Their bite is highly venomous.

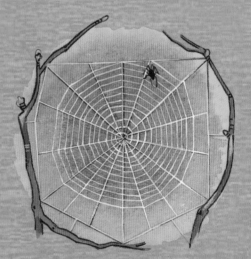

Stage 3
The spider fills the frame with circular threads.

All about legs

Centipedes and millipedes have hundreds of legs and belong to the myriapod group. Worms, snails and slugs have no legs, so they are not insects. They get around by sliding their bodies along the ground.

Slither and slime
Snails and slugs leave slimy trails wherever they have been. The slime is used for protection and to create a smooth surface for movement.

Burrowing deep down

Earthworms are good for soil. When they burrow into the ground, they allow extra air to reach the roots of plants. This helps the plants to grow.

Make a wormery

You will need

see-through container • sand • soil • leaves • worms

1 In a see-through container, put a 5-centimetre layer of sand and then a 5-centimetre layer of soil. Alternate the sand and soil until your container is almost full. Add leaves to the top.

2 Add some worms from your garden to the container, and keep it in a cool, dark place.

3 Every few days, see how the worms mix up the layers. Carefully put the worms back where you found them when you've finished.

Leeches have suckers at the end of their bodies for sucking blood.

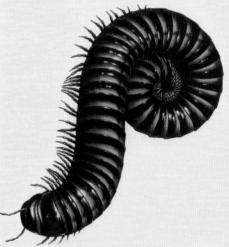

The **Giant African millipede** can grow up to 28 centimetres long.

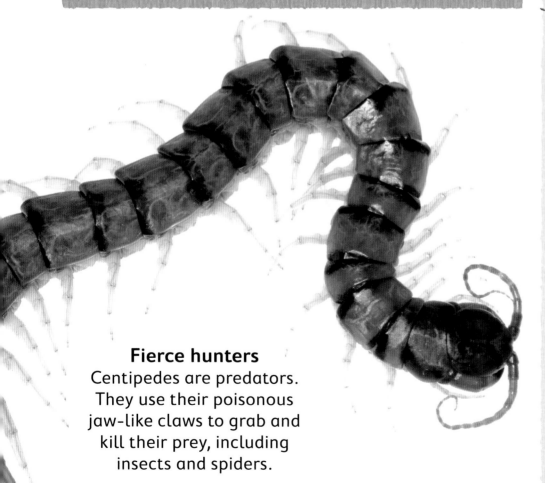

Fierce hunters
Centipedes are predators. They use their poisonous jaw-like claws to grab and kill their prey, including insects and spiders.

When disturbed, **pill millipedes** curl into a ball to protect themselves.

Life on the Nile

Without the river Nile, Egyptian civilization might never have existed. The Nile provided water for transport, drinking and watering crops.

Boats were the best way to get around in Egypt

Papyrus reeds had many uses, including making boats and shoes

Living on the Nile

Most Egyptians lived on the river's banks so they could grow crops. People spread further along the Nile as Egypt became more powerful.

Blocks of stone for the pyramids were carried across the river

Every June the Nile **flooded**, covering the land with a dark soil in which farmers planted crops.

The Nile carried **boats** laden with animals and goods, some of which were traded on the banks.

Water was taken from the Nile using a **shaduf** — a wooden bucket hanging from a long pole.

149

Powerful pharaohs

The rulers of ancient Egypt were called pharaohs. Ordinary people believed that they were gods. The pharaoh was the most important and powerful person in the country.

Gods and goddesses

The ancient Egyptians worshipped more than 1000 different gods and goddesses. The most important was Ra, the sun god. A god was often shown as an animal, or half-human, half-animal.

Ra   *Osiris*   *Anubis*

Isis

Who's in charge

Officials called viziers helped the pharaoh to rule Egypt. Each ruler chose two viziers. They were very powerful and important men.

Queen Hatshepsut

Hatshepsut was crowned pharaoh in 1473 BC when her husband, Thutmose II, died. She adopted the royal symbols of the double crown, the crook, the flail (whip) — and also the ceremonial beard!

Ramses II ruled for more than 60 years. He was a great builder and a brave soldier.

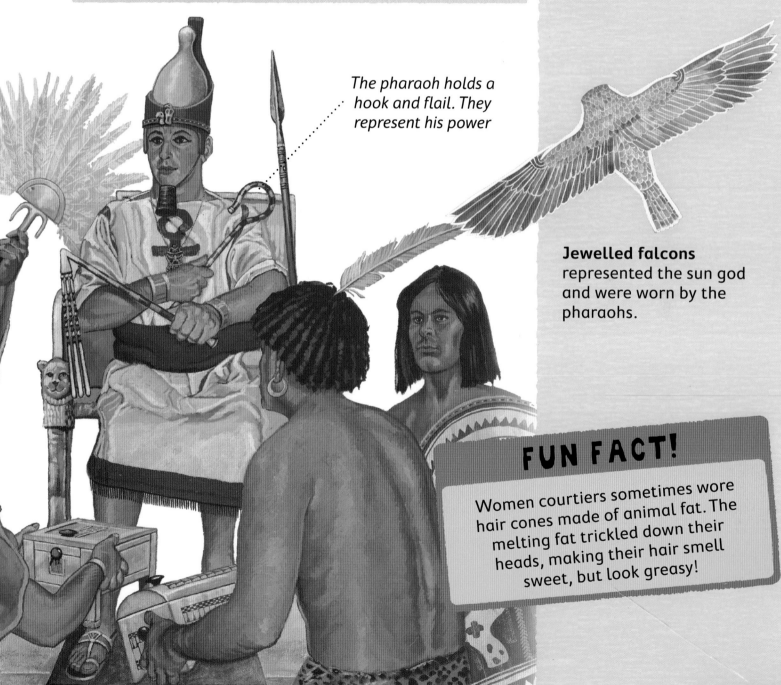

The pharaoh holds a hook and flail. They represent his power

Jewelled falcons represented the sun god and were worn by the pharaohs.

FUN FACT!

Women courtiers sometimes wore hair cones made of animal fat. The melting fat trickled down their heads, making their hair smell sweet, but look greasy!

The pyramids of Giza

The three pyramids at Giza are more than 4500 years old. They were built for three kings — Khufu, Khafre and Menkaure. After they died, their bodies were preserved as mummies and buried inside the pyramids.

The finished pyramids had a white coating to protect the stones underneath

Blocks of stone were moved by wooden sledges

The workers were given lots of water while working in the hot desert

152

The biggest pyramid

The Great Pyramid is the biggest pyramid in the world. It was built with more than two million blocks.

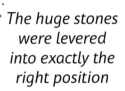

The huge stones were levered into exactly the right position

The **Great Sphinx at Giza** has the body of a lion and the head of a human.

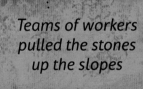

Teams of workers pulled the stones up the slopes

Breaking in

Tomb robbers broke into the pyramids to steal the treasures that were buried with the pharaohs.

The **Step Pyramid** is one of the world's oldest pyramids.

153

Temples and tombs

The ancient Egyptians built magnificent buildings, including temples and tombs. From 2150 BC, pharaohs were not buried in pyramids, but in tombs in the Valley of the Kings. Gods such as Ra were worshipped in temples.

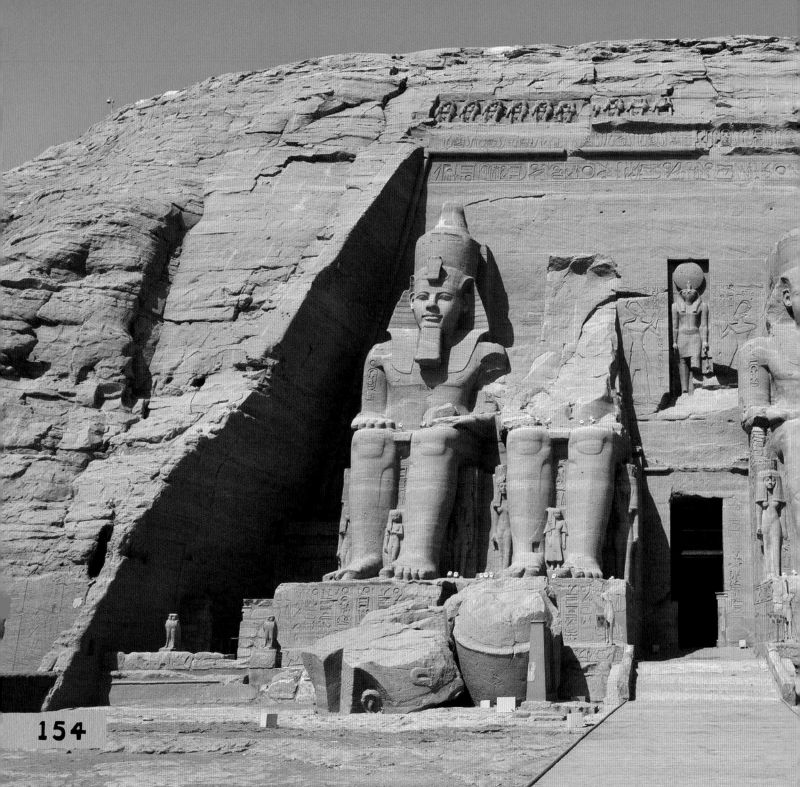

Canopic jars were used to store the dead person's body parts

The priest wore a jackal mask to look like the god Anubis

In 1922 the **death mask** of Tutankhamun was found in the Valley of the Kings.

Preserving the dead

Dead bodies were turned into mummies. The insides were removed and the body was left to dry for 40 days. Then it was washed, filled with linen, covered in oil and finally wrapped in linen bandages.

The riches in the **Valley of the Kings** attracted many tomb robbers.

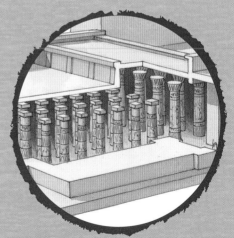

The temple of Osiris

The temple at Abu Simbel is carved out of sandstone rock. Four enormous statues of Ramses II guard the entrance. They are more than 20 metres high.

The **Great Hall at Karnak** has 134 papyrus columns that are up to 21 metres tall.

The working life

Most people worked as craftworkers or farm labourers, including potters, carpenters, weavers, jewellers and shoemakers. Scribes were important people because they knew how to read and write. They kept records of daily events.

Working for the pharaoh
Craftworkers had special areas within the town where they produced statues and furniture for the pharaoh.

Life at home

Egyptian houses were made from mud bricks. Inside walls were covered with thick plaster, which kept them cool in the heat. Wealthy families lived in country villas. Poorer families lived in a crowded single room.

Senet was a popular board game

Children played with wooden or clay toys

The Egyptians used woven papyrus mats instead of carpets

Workers often made a living by selling their goods at the market.

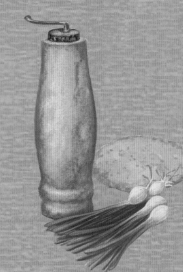

A **typical lunch** for a worker was bread and onions, washed down with beer.

Becoming a scribe

Only the sons of scribes went to school to learn how to read and write. Then they could be scribes, too.

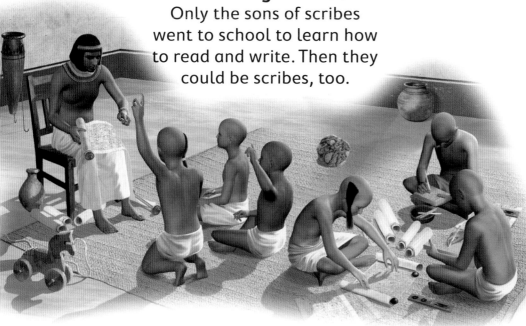

Bread was an important part of every meal. Loaves came in all shapes and sizes and were cooked on a hot oven.

Painting words

The ancient Egyptians used a system of picture-writing called hieroglyphics. Each hieroglyph, or picture, represented an object or sound. The insides of tombs were decorated with hieroglyphs, often showing scenes from the dead person's life.

Painting tombs
Several artists worked together to paint tombs with colourful symbols and scenes. The Egyptians believed the scenes would come to life in the next world.

A junior artist drew the outlines of the scenes

A senior artist checked and corrected the outlines, then painted over them in black paint

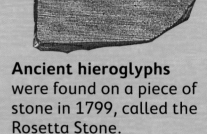

Write your name in hieroglyphics

Below is the hieroglyphic alphabet. You can use it to write your name or letters to your friends.

A B C D E F G H I

J K L M N O P Q R

S T U V W X Y Z

Ancient hieroglyphs were found on a piece of stone in 1799, called the Rosetta Stone.

The hieroglyphs of a ruler's name were written inside an **oval frame**.

A painter filled in the outlines in colour

FUN FACT!

Schoolchildren had to learn 700 different hieroglyphs.

159

The Roman Empire

An empire is made up of many different countries ruled by one person — the emperor. Rome in Italy was once the centre of a great empire. It became rich and powerful, ruling more than 50 million people around the world.

Key

1 Slaves captured during battle were tied up and walked through the city.

2 Soldiers marched through Rome to celebrate a victory at war.

3 The emperor led the victory parade on a golden chariot.

Capital city
More than one million people lived in Rome and by AD 300, it was the largest city in the world.

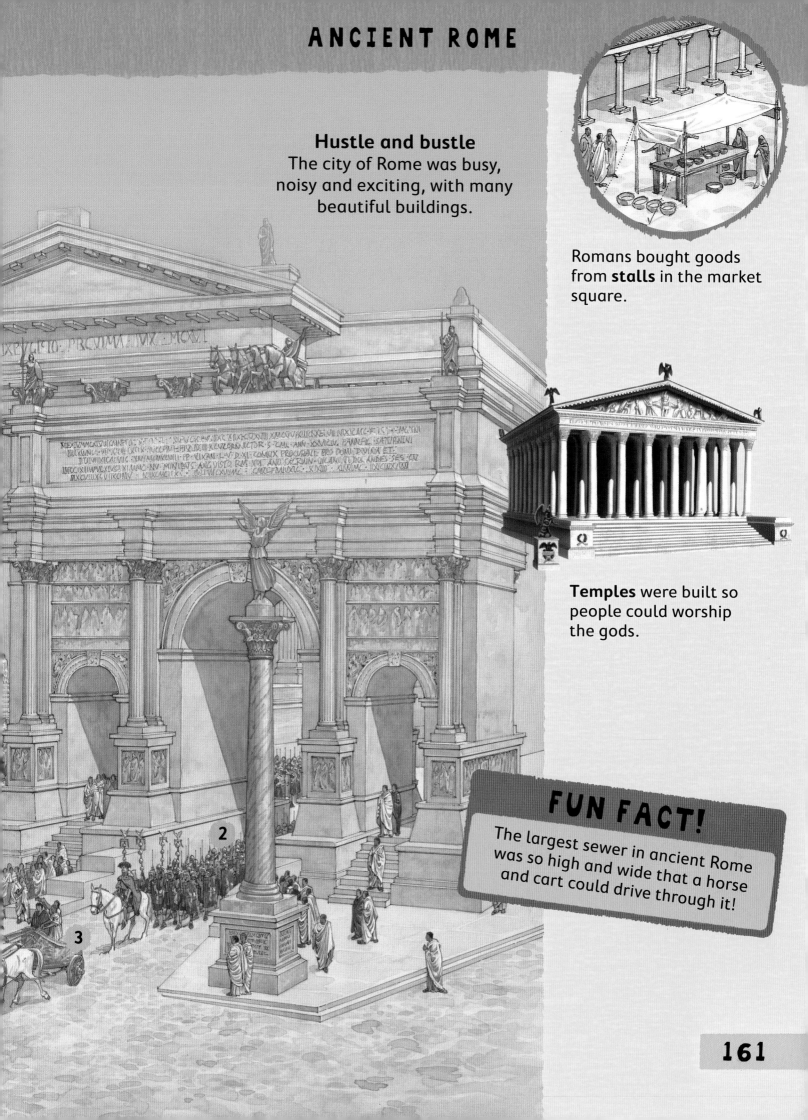

Hustle and bustle
The city of Rome was busy, noisy and exciting, with many beautiful buildings.

Romans bought goods from **stalls** in the market square.

Temples were built so people could worship the gods.

FUN FACT!
The largest sewer in ancient Rome was so high and wide that a horse and cart could drive through it!

161

Rulers of Rome

For a long time, Rome was ruled by kings. It became a republic – a state without a king – after many years of fighting. An army general called Octavian took power and became the first emperor, bringing peace to Rome.

Julius Caesar
In 47 BC, a successful general called Julius Caesar declared himself dictator. His reign ended in 44 BC when he was killed.

Roman law
Everyone in Rome had to obey the laws, which were very strict. If someone was accused of a serious crime, they attended court to see if they were innocent or guilty.

Senators worked for the government. They made new laws

Mars, god of war and Venus, goddess of love

Neptune, god of the sea

Jupiter, king of the gods and Juno, queen of the gods

Roman coins showed the most powerful people of the time, usually the emperor.

Gods and goddesses

The Romans worshipped many gods and goddesses. Some were believed to protect Rome, and the emperor offered sacrifices to them.

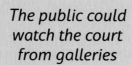

The public could watch the court from galleries

Octavian became the first Roman emperor in 27 BC. He introduced many laws.

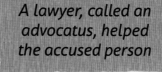

A lawyer, called an advocatus, helped the accused person

A person accused of a crime had to go to court

FUN FACT!

The mad Emperor Nero was said to have laughed and played music while watching a terrible fire destroy part of Rome.

The people of Rome

By around AD 300, Rome was the largest city in the world. The government was run by rich nobles and knights. Ordinary citizens were poor, but they could vote and serve in the army. Slaves had no rights at all.

The Forum

At the heart of the city was a large marketplace called the Forum. It was surrounded by government buildings. People went to the Forum to meet their friends and people they worked with, to listen to famous speakers, or to talk with others about important matters.

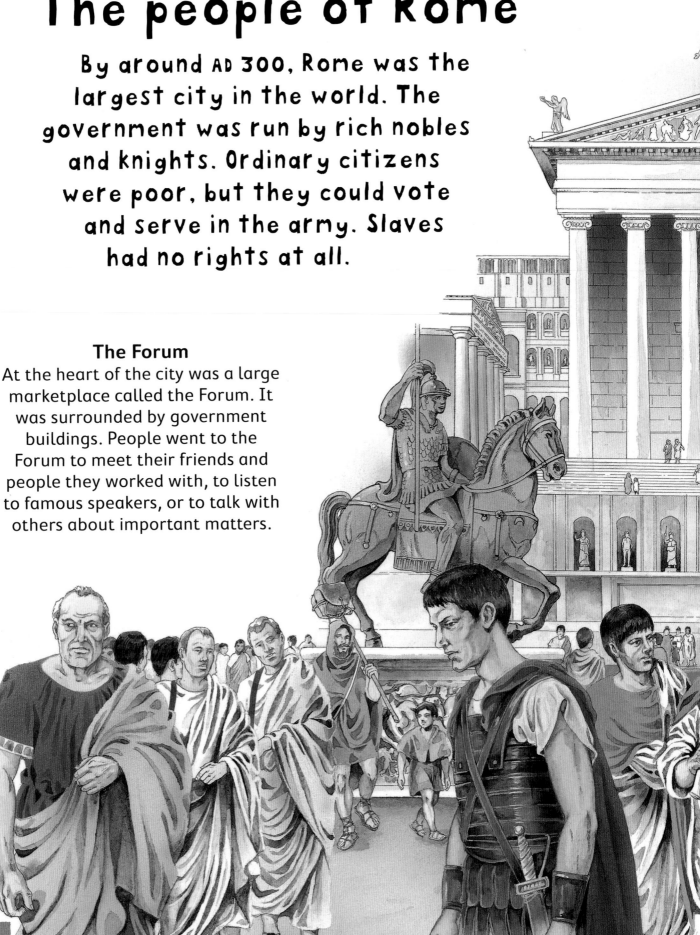

Slave trade

Slaves were bought and sold at slave-markets. They were shown to the citizens to be chosen or rejected. Sometimes they were set free by their owners.

City guards protected Rome from outside attackers.

Senators were important government leaders.

FUN FACT!

Roman engineers also designed public lavatories. These lavatories were not private. Users sat on rows of seats, side by side!

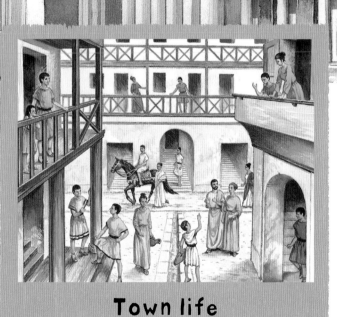

Town life

In cities, many Romans lived in blocks of flats called 'insulae'.

A trip to the baths

Roman baths were places to wash, relax, meet friends and get fit. Visitors could have a massage or a haircut. They could also buy scented oils and perfumes, read a book, eat, or admire works of art.

Luxury baths
One of the most popular baths was at Aquae Sulis (Bath). It had changing rooms and lockers, as well as hot, warm and cold baths.

The Great Bath was adorned with statues

Hot springs
The Romans believed that the heat of the water used at Aquae Sulis was the mystical work of the gods. Now we know that the water source was an ancient hot spring.

Today only the actual water bath at Aquae Sulis is original, the other buildings date from the 18th century

Luxury baths

The Baths of Caracalla in Rome included not only baths but libraries, shops and gardens that covered a total of 25 hectares.

Fires heated the water for the hot rooms.

The **tepidarium** had a cool or lukewarm pool.

Men and women did not bathe together. Women usually went to the baths in the mornings, while men were at work. Men went in the afternoons.

167

The mighty Colosseum

The Colosseum was a huge oval arena in the centre of Rome, which could seat 50,000 people. It was built of stone, concrete and marble and had 80 separate entrances. It was used for gladiator fights and pretend sea battles.

Gladiator battles

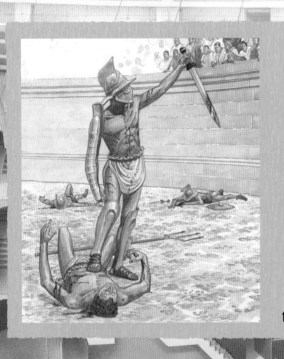

Gladiators had to fight in the arena until they died. A wounded fighter pleads for his life by showing a thumbs-up sign. If the crowd thought he should die, the people showed a thumbs-down sign.

6

5

ANCIENT ROME

Colosseum key

1 Awning (canvas roof)
2 Tiered seating
3 Arena floor
4 Trapdoor
5 Underground tunnels
6 Stairs leading to seating areas

Gladiator **helmets** were decorated with plumes and crests to make them look taller or bigger.

Gladiator battles
The Colosseum could seat 50,000 people to watch the games. The first games lasted 100 days.

Gladiators were named after a short, stabbing sword called the **gladius**.

FUN FACT!
Gladiators became so popular that people wrote graffiti about them on the walls of buildings around Rome.

In the army

The Roman Empire needed troops to defend its land against enemy attack. It was a dangerous job, but the soldiers were well paid and cared for. After around 25 years of service, they were given money or land.

Tortoise shell

During battles, soldiers used their shields to make a protective 'shell' called a testudo, or tortoise. Their shields were placed at all sides.

FUN FACT!

Roman soldiers kept warm in cold countries by wearing woolly underpants beneath their tunics!

Roman roads

Rome was at the centre of a road network that stretched over 85,000 kilometres, making it easier for the army and leaders to move around the empire.

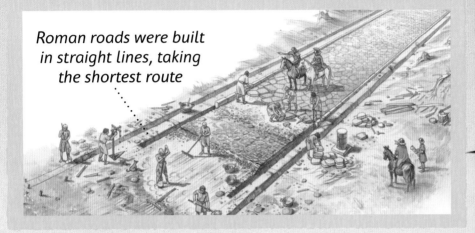

Roman roads were built in straight lines, taking the shortest route

On the move

The Roman army marched around the empire to where they were needed. They travelled up to 30 kilometres a day!

Roman cavalry soldiers rode horses and helped the foot soldiers during battle.

Roman armour was made from metal strips held together by straps and buckles.

The most important travellers on the roads were **official messengers** who rode on horseback.

Life in the Middle Ages

In the Middle Ages, between **470** and **1450**, many
castles and forts were built. A castle provided
shelter for a king or lord and his family,
and helped him to defend his lands.

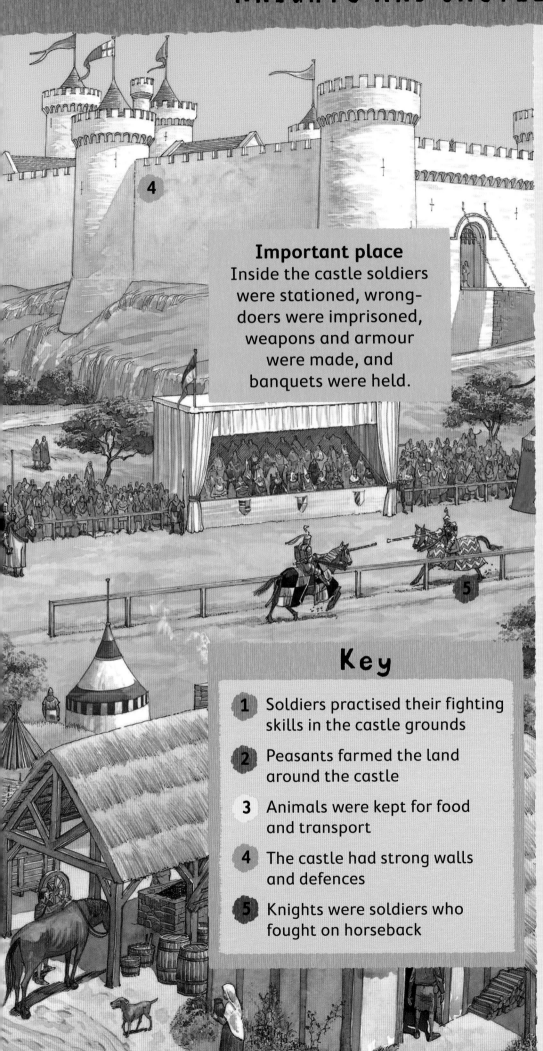

The **drawbridge** was the entrance to the castle.

Important place
Inside the castle soldiers were stationed, wrong-doers were imprisoned, weapons and armour were made, and banquets were held.

Banquets (feasts) were held in the **Great Hall**.

Key

1 Soldiers practised their fighting skills in the castle grounds

2 Peasants farmed the land around the castle

3 Animals were kept for food and transport

4 The castle had strong walls and defences

5 Knights were soldiers who fought on horseback

The lord and his family had a private living area called the **solar**.

Building castles

The best place to build a castle was on top of a hill. A hilltop position gave good views over the surrounding countryside, making it harder for an enemy to launch a surprise attack.

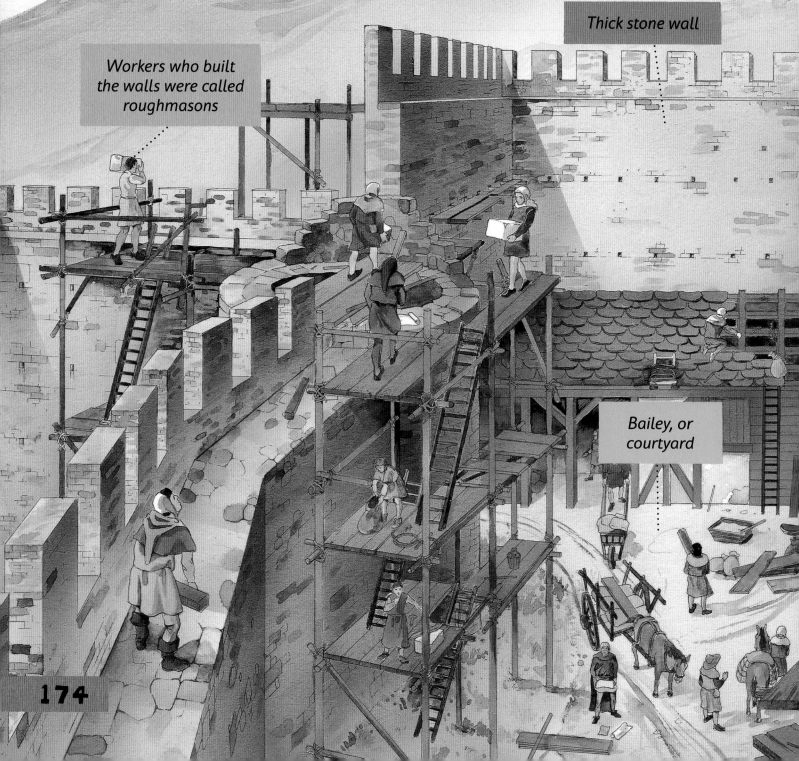

Thick stone wall

Workers who built the walls were called roughmasons

Bailey, or courtyard

174

The keep was the safest part of the castle, where the lord lived

Waterworks
Inside the castle was a bailey (courtyard) with a thick wall around it. Most castles got water from a well inside the bailey. Water was drawn up with a large water wheel.

Water wheel

The master mason was in charge of the workers

Well

The **keep** had banquet rooms and bedrooms for the lord and his family.

Heavy materials were placed in buckets and pulled up to where they were needed.

Workers carried stones, dug trenches and mixed mortar (sand and water).

Inside the castle

Stone castles were cold, damp places. Cold winds blew through the windows, which had no glass. There was no heating or running water.

House and home

The lord and lady did not live inside the castle alone. Servants and knights also had their own quarters. Even prisoners stayed in the castle – in the dungeon.

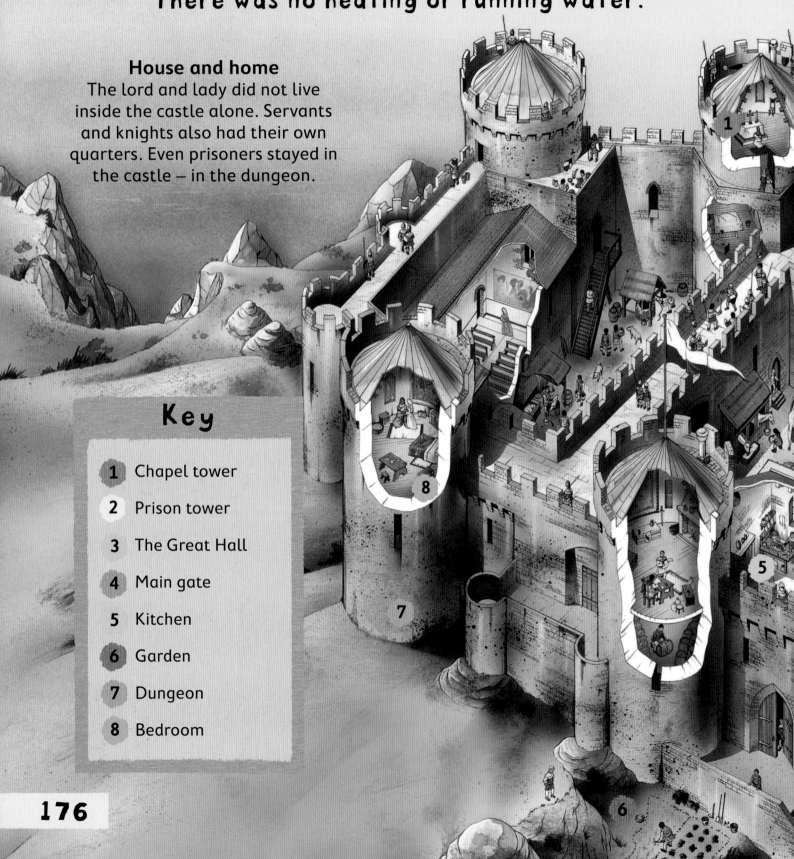

Key

1 Chapel tower

2 Prison tower

3 The Great Hall

4 Main gate

5 Kitchen

6 Garden

7 Dungeon

8 Bedroom

Design a castle

You will need:
pencil • paper • colouring pens

1 Draw a plan of your ideal castle, making sure it has plenty of defences. Will it have arrow slits? Will the walls be high? Will it have a moat running around it?

2 Don't forget to design a drawbridge to let the lord and his family in and out of their castle.

Servants cooked, cleaned and ran errands.

A **blacksmith** (right) made shoes for all the horses. An **armourer** made weapons and armour for the army.

Local **villagers** were allowed to shelter inside the castle walls when their lands were under attack.

Nobles and knights

In the Middle Ages, the king or queen was the most important person in the country. The king or queen gave land to noblemen in return for soldiers and weapons to fight wars. From the age of seven, the sons of noblemen were trained to become knights.

Knights in training

It took 14 years to become a knight. First, boys were taught to ride horses and shoot arrows. Then they became squires (assistants), and learned to fight with swords. If they were good enough, they became knights at the age of 21.

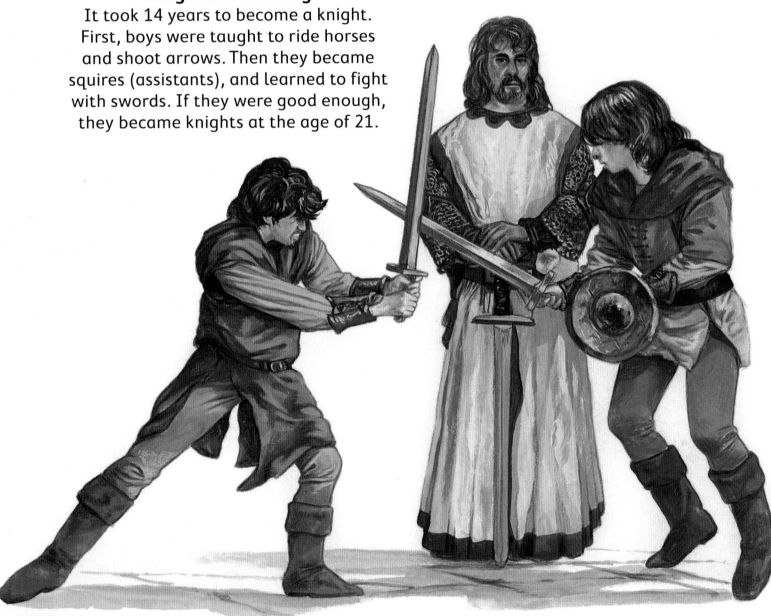

Swords with two sharp edges were used by knights in the Middle Ages.

The dubbing ceremony
The ceremony of making a new knight was known as dubbing. A knight had to pray all night in church before his dubbing ceremony took place.

A mace had deadly spikes to pierce armour.

A new knight
During the dubbing ceremony, a lord or another knight tapped the new knight on the shoulder with a sword.

A rich knight had three horses for fighting, riding and carrying heavy loads.

179

Jousting tournaments

Knights often took part in pretend battles called tournaments. Tournaments were good practice for the real thing — war. Knights divided into two sides and fought each other as if in a proper battle.

Knights aimed to hit their opponent's head, chest or shield with their lance

Lances were made of metal. Their tips were not sharp, so knights didn't get seriously injured

Create your own shield

You will need
coloured pens • paper

1 Draw a big shield shape on a piece of paper.

2 On the shield, draw a symbol for your family — perhaps swords or a crown.

3 Colour in your shield, then hang it on your bedroom door to show everyone that you're a knight!

In competition

Jousting was a fight between two knights on horseback. Each knight tried to win by knocking the other off his horse.

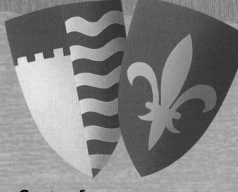

A wooden rail separated the two riders. If a knight fell, the rail stopped him from being trodden on by the other horse

Coats of arms were badges worn by knights so others could recognize them.

Banners displayed a knight's own personal design.

FUN FACT!

Some knights cheated in jousts by wearing special armour that was fixed onto the horse's saddle!

Into battle

Battles were fought to end disagreements or to gain land, wealth and power. Knights and soldiers fought for the lord. In return, the lord looked after them or gave them land.

Building defences
Knights marched or rode into battle carrying the flag and coat of arms of their lord. Ordinary soldiers fought on foot.

Dress for battle

Early knights wore chainmail — armour made of many tiny iron rings joined to each other. By the 1400s, suits of armour were made of steel plates.

Gauntlets (steel-plated gloves)

Helmets

Shield

Knights with **armoured horses** were put on the front row during battle.

Weapons at the ready

Knights had two main weapons — the sword and the shield. They also fought with lances (long wooden spears), daggers and axes.

Some **knights** used a weapon called the morning star — a spiked ball on the end of a chain.

FUN FACT!

Soldiers called 'retrievers' had to run into the middle of the battle and collect all the spare arrows!

Castle siege

A siege is when an enemy surrounds a castle and stops all supplies from reaching the people inside. The idea is to starve them until they surrender or die.

Attack!

An attacking enemy needed to break through the castle's defences to get inside the walls. Knights and soldiers used as many weapons as possible, including giant catapults.

The trebuchet fired stones using an arm with a sling

Knights surrounded the castle, waiting for the enemy to surrender

This gigantic catapult fired large rocks at the walls

Inside a tower called a belfry, attackers could reach the top of the wall safely

Attackers climbed ladders to try to get into the castle quickly

The battering ram was a heavy log used to attack gates and walls

FUN FACT!

The ropes used to wind up trebuchet machines were made from plaits of human hair!

Attackers dug **tunnels** under walls and towers. They then lit fires to make the towers collapse.

Attackers were protected from arrows inside the **battering ram**.

Fighting back

An attacking enemy had to break through a castle's defences to get inside its walls. Defenders would pull up the castle drawbridge and lower an iron gate, called a portcullis.

Keeping them out
Defenders of the castle used many different methods to try to keep out their enemies. They threw stone missiles, fired arrows and even poured boiling water over the castle walls.

Key

1 Battlements along the top of the walls gave soldiers something to hide behind

2 The thick stone wall was difficult for attackers to break down

3 Heavy stones were thrown onto the enemy below

4 Archers fired arrows at the attackers

5 Boiling water was poured onto the heads of enemies

Archers would fire arrows at the enemy through **narrow slits** in the castle walls.

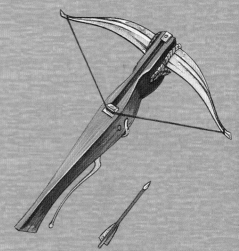

A **crossbow** was a more accurate weapon than a bow and arrow.

Archers stood on the castle walls and fired down at enemies.

187

INDEX

A

Abu Simbel temple 155
Age of Dinosaurs 72
agoutis 107
air 15
air pressure 44
algae 33
Allosaurus 73
Ankylosaurus 80, 81
Antarctic 85
Antarctic birds 128, 129
Antarctic mammals 102
Antarctic penguins 120
ants 136, 137
Apatosaurus 71
apes 106
apollo butterfly 139
Aquae Sulis, Bath 166
arachnids 132, 133, 144
archers 186, 187
Arctic 85
Arctic birds 128, 129
Arctic mammals 102
Arctic tern 95, 121
Argentinosaurus 71
armour 171, 177, 181, 183
armoured dinosaurs 80, 89
asteroids 6
astronauts 7
astronomers 19
atmosphere of the Earth
  13, 23, 42
atmospheres of the
  planets 11
atom bomb 54
atoms 58, 66, 67
autumn 41
aye-aye 107

B

baby birds 116, 117
baby dinosaurs 78, 79
baby mammals 98, 99
bailey 175
bald eagle 118, 125
baleen 105
banded sea snakes 87
banners 181
banquets 173
barnacles 85
Barosaurus 70

barreleye fish 89
Baths of Caracalla, Rome
  167
bats 106
battering ram 185
battery 59
battlements 186
bears 112
Beaufort scale 44
beavers 97
bee-eater 122
bees 134, 135
beetles 135, 137, 142, 143
bird flight 115
birds 114, 115
birds' beaks 122, 123
birds' eggs 114, 116, 117
birds' nests 118, 119
birds of prey 124, 125
birds swimming 120, 121
birds' wings 115
blacksmith 177
block mountains 29
blue bird of paradise 126
blue whale 99, 104
bottlenose dolphin 84
Brachiosaurus 71
breccia 25
breeze 44
brown bears 112
bugs 132, 133
butterflies 139

C

cables 58, 59
camels 108
cameras 53
camouflage 90
candles 50, 51
caracals 113
carbon fibre 64
carnivore mammals 112
castle building 174, 175
castle defences 186, 187
castle rooms 175
castle siege 184, 185
catapults 184
caterpillars 143
cave crickets 137
caves 34, 35
cave swiftlets 119

centipedes 133, 146, 147
ceramics 65
chainmail 183
chalk 25
chambers 34
cheetah 113
chicks 116
chimpanzee 99
circuits 59
cirrus clouds 43
civets 106
click beetles 141
climates 38
clouds 29, 42, 43, 46
coats of arms 181, 182
cochlea 55
cockchafer beetles 135
cockroaches 140
Coelophysis 77
coins of Rome 163
cold-blooded creatures
  86, 87
cold temperate climate
  39
colonies 136
Colosseum, Rome 168,
  169
colours 52
computers 62, 63
conduction 51
cone-shaped volcanoes
  27
constellations 19
continental crust 25
continents 15, 23
convection 51
core 25
corona 9
Corythosaurus 75
cotton 65
craters 12, 23
crater volcanoes 27
Cretaceous Period 68
crickets 137, 141
crocodiles 87
crossbows 187
crust 24, 25, 30
crystals 35
cuckoos 119
cumulonimbus clouds 43
cyclones 45

D

death's head hawk moths
  143
decibel scale 54
deep-sea creatures 88, 89
delta 32
desert climate 38
desert kangaroo rat 109
desert mammals 108, 109
deserts 39
desktop computer 62
dinosaur brains 74, 75
dinosaur eggs 78, 79, 83
dinosaur eyesight 74
dinosaur hearing 74
dinosaur nests 78
dinosaur speeds 76
Diplodocus 71
dippers 130
dogs 112, 113
dolphins 84, 96, 104, 105
dragonflies 139
drawbridge 173, 186
dry temperate climate 39
dubbing 179
duck-billed platypus 98,
  101
ducklings 117
ducks 121
dugongs 85
dung beetles 142
dungeon 176
dusky dolphin 96

E

eagles 121, 124, 125
eardrums 55
early dinosaurs 68, 69
ears 55
earthquakes 30, 31
Earth's formation 22, 23
Earth's seasons 40
Earth's structure 25
Earth's surface 7
Earth's water cycle 42
earthworms 146
earwigs 135
echo 55
eclipse 9
Edmontonia 81
eels 95

INDEX

egg tooth 116
Egyptian gods and goddesses 150
Egyptians 148, 149
Egyptian vulture 122
Egyptian workers 156, 157
Egyptian writing 158, 159
electrical energy 49, 60
electricity 58, 59
electricity and magnetism 56
electricity generation 45
electricity in lightning 46
electromagnet 56, 57
electrons 58, 66
elephants 99
elliptical galaxies 21
emperor penguin 117, 120
emperors 162, 163
emu 117
energy in chemicals 50
energy in electricity 49, 58
energy in light 52
energy in stars 19
engine 54
epicentre 30, 31
Equator 38, 39
Euoplocephalus 81
European bee-eater 122
evaporation 42
Everest 29

F

fangtooth fish 89
fault line 30, 31
feathers 114, 115
fennec fox 109
fireflies 139
fireworks 50
fish 90, 91
flash floods 42
fleas 141
flooding 42
flounders 90
flying fish 91
focus 30, 31
fog 43
fold mountains 28, 29
forces 48, 56, 57
forked lightning 47

forts 172
Forum, Rome 164
fossils 69, 74, 75, 82
froghoppers 143
funnelweb spiders 145
fur 102, 103
furniture beetles 143

G

gadgets 48
galaxies 13, 20, 21
gales 44
Galilean moons 17
Galileo Galilei 17
gallery 35
gannets 121
gas 8, 18, 19
gassy planets 16
generators 45, 59
gentoo penguin 121
gerbils 108
giant clams 88
giant isopods 89
giant squid 89
giant tube worms 88
Giganotosaurus 73
gills 90
giraffe 111
Giza Pyramids, Egypt 152, 153
glaciers 36, 37
glacier valley 37
gladiator fights 168, 169
gladius 169
glass 65
gods and goddesses 150, 163
golden eagle 124
gorillas 99
grasshoppers 140, 141
gravity 10, 18, 48
great diving beetle 137
Great Pyramid of Giza 153
Great Red Spot 16
Great Sphinx 153
green turtle 87
grey parrots 127
grey whale 105
guillemot 117
gulper eel 89

H

hailstones 47
harp seal 103
hatching 116
hawks 124, 125
hawksbill turtle 87
headphone socket 62
hearing 55
heat 50, 51
helium 67
helmets 169
herons 131
Herrerasaurus 68
hieroglyphics 158, 159
Himalayas 29
hippopotamus 100, 101
hives 134
honeybee 134
hornbills 115
houseflies 132
hummingbirds 123
humpback whale 95, 105
hunting dogs 113
hurricane 44, 45
hyacinth macaw 127
hydrogen 67
hyenas 109

I

ice 36, 37, 47
icebergs 36
incubation 117
inner core 25
insect flight 138, 139
insect homes 136, 137
insect nests 134, 135, 137
insect wings 138
Internet 63
Io 17
iPad 63
iron 56, 57
irregular galaxies 21

J

jacanas 131
jaguar 106
jet engines 54
jousting 180, 181
Julius Caesar 162
Jupiter 6, 10, 11, 16, 17
Jurassic Period 68

K

Karnak Temple 155
keep 175
keyboard 62
killer whale 105
kingfisher 130
King Khafre 152
King Kufu 152
King Menkaure 152

L

ladybirds 135, 138
lakes 32, 33, 42
lances 180
laptop computer 62
lava 27, 28
lava bombs 26
Leaellynasaura 74
leafcutter ants 136
leafhoppers 141
leeches 147
lemurs 107, 111
leopard seal 92, 93
light 52, 53
lightning 46, 47
light rays 52
light waves 53, 60
limestone 25
lions 112
loggerhead turtle 94
loudspeakers 55
lower mantle 25

M

Maat Mons volcano 15
macaws 126, 127
maces 179
machines 48
Maglev trains 57
magma 25
magma chamber 26, 27
magnetic energy 60
magnetic field 57
magnetism 56, 57
Maiasaura 78, 79
manatees 101
mantle 25
marine iguana 86
Mars 10, 11, 14, 15
materials 64, 65

meander 33
meat-eating dinosaurs 68, 69, 72, 73
meltwater 37
memory stick 63
Mercury 10, 11, 12, 14, 15
Mesozoic Era 68
metal 64
Meteor Crater 23
meteorites 23, 82
mice 63
microchips 63
microwaves 60, 61
Middle Ages 172, 173
migration 94
milk 97, 98
Milky Way 20, 21
millipedes 133, 146, 147
minerals 33, 34, 35
mites 133
mobile phones 63
molluscs 133
monitor screen 62
monkeys 106
Moon 9, 10, 11, 12, 23
moons of Jupiter 17
moons of Mars 15
mosquitoes 139
mountaineers 29
mountain lion 98
mountains 24, 28, 32, 38, 39
mouthparts 132
mummies 152, 155
mushroom stones 37
musk ox 103
Muttaburrasaurus 77
myriapods 133, 146, 147

N

nebulae 13, 18
Neptune 10, 16, 17
Nero 163
neutrons 66, 67
noblemen 178
North Pole 38, 40, 41, 84
Northern Hemisphere seasons 40, 41
nucleus 66
nuthatches 123

O

oarfish 91
ocean migrations 94
oceans 12, 15, 23, 42
Octavian 162, 163
orang-utans 97
orbits 10, 40
Ornithomimus 76, 77
osprey 131
ostrich 115
outer core 25
owls 124
oxbow lake 33
oxpeckers 123
oxygen 67

P

panda 110
pangolins 97
papyrus reeds 148
Parasaurolophus 75
pelicans 131
penguins 120, 128
pharaohs 150, 151
pharaohs' tombs 154, 155
Philippine eagle 124
Phobos 15
pigeons 115
pill millipedes 133, 147
planet Earth 10, 11, 12, 13, 15
planets 10, 22
plant-eating dinosaurs 69
plant-eating mammals 110
plants 15
plastic 64, 65
plates (Earth's crust) 30
platypus 98, 101
polar bear 84, 102
polar climate 39
Poles (Earth's) 38, 40, 41, 84
poles of a magnet 57
portcullis 186
pottos 106
power stations 58, 59
pregnancy 99
prism 52
protons 66, 67
ptarmigan 129

puffin 123
puma 98
pylons 58, 59
pyramids 149, 152, 153

Q

Queen Hatshepsut 151
quetzals 127

R

rabbits 111
radios 60, 61
radio waves 60, 61
rain 38, 42, 43
rainbow 52
rainbow lorikeet 127
rainforest 39
rainforest birds 126, 127
rainforest mammals 106, 107
rainwater 34, 35
Rameses II 151, 155
Ra, the Sun god 150, 151, 154
rat tail fish 88
raven 125
redback spider 144
red panda 97
red stars 19
reflection 53
refraction 53
reptiles 68, 74, 78, 86
republic of Rome 162
rhinoceros 111
Richter scale 31
rings of planets 11, 16, 17
ring-tailed lemur 107
river birds 130, 131
river Nile 148, 149
river otter 100
rivers 32, 33, 42, 43
rock cycle 24
rockets 7
rocks 24, 25, 34
rocky planets 14
Roman army 170, 171
Roman baths 166, 167
Roman Empire 160, 161
Roman gods and goddesses 163
Roman people 164, 165

Roman roads 171
rookeries 120
Rosetta Stone 159
rubber 64

S

salmon 95
Saltopus 69
saltwater crocodile 87
sand wasps 143
Sarawak Chamber, Malaysia 35
satellites 60
Saturn 10, 11, 16
sauropods 70, 71
scarlet macaw 126
school of fish 90
schools of dolphins 104
science 48, 49
scorpionfly 135
scorpions 109
scribes 156, 157
sea 42
sea lions 92, 93, 104
seals 85, 92, 99, 103, 104
sea otter 93
seas 12
sea snakes 87
seasons 40, 41
secretary bird 124
senators of Rome 165
sense of smell 74
shaduf 149
sharks 91
sheet lightning 47
shields 170, 180
shield volcanoes 27
shockwaves 30, 31
sieges 184, 185
skyscrapers 49
slaves 165
sloths 107
slugs 146
snails 133, 146
snouts (of glaciers) 36
snow 29, 38
snow bunting 129
snow leopard 103
snow mammals 102, 103
snowshoe hare 103
snowy owl 129

solar eclipses 9
solar flares 8
solar panels 59
solar prominences 8, 9
Solar System 10
soldiers, Roman 170, 171
sound 54, 55
southern elephant seal 93
South Pole 38, 40
space 6
space exploration 49
speaking 55
spectrum 52
sperm whale 84
spiders 144, 145
spider webs 145
Spinosaurus 73, 80
spiny lobster 95
spiral galaxies 21
spittlebugs 143
spring 32, 33, 40
stalactites 34, 35
stalagmites 34, 35
stars 8, 13, 18, 19, 22
steel 56, 57
Step Pyramid 153
storks 131
storm 45
stratus clouds 43
stream 32, 33
Struthiomimus 77
subatomic particles 66
summer 40, 41
Sun 8, 9, 10, 11, 19, 22, 40, 42
sunfish 91
sunshine 38
sunspots 8, 9
swallows 119
swans 115, 129
swimming mammals 104, 105
swords 169, 178, 179

T

tablets 63
talking 54
talons 124
tapirs 107
tarantula spider 144

television 60, 61
temperate climate 38
temperate (grassland climate) 39
temples 154, 155, 161
tepidarium 167
termites 137, 143
testudo 170
thermometer 51
thunder 46, 47, 54
ticks 132
tiger 112, 113
tomb robbers 153, 155
tombs, Egyptian 154, 155, 158
total eclipse 9
toucans 127
touchpads 62
tournaments 180
transport 49
trebuchets 184
Triassic Period 68
Triceratops 81
Troodon 74, 75
tropical forest climate 38
tropical grassland climate 39
tropical storms 45
tsunamis 31
tundra swan 129
turtle eggs 87
turtles 87, 94
tusks 103
Tutankhamun 155
typhoon 45
Tyrannosaurus rex 72, 73, 75

U

upper mantle 25
Uranus 10, 16, 17

V

Valdivia earthquake, Chile 31
valleys 37
Valley of the Kings 154, 155
vent crabs 88
Venus 10, 11, 12, 14, 15
Virginia opossum 99

volcanoes 15, 17, 23, 25, 26, 27, 28, 83
vultures 122, 123

W

wading birds 131
walruses 92, 93, 103
warm-blooded mammals 84, 92, 96
wasps 137
water 15
water cycle 42, 43
waterfalls 33, 34, 35
water opossum 100
water rat 100
water vapour 42, 43
water vole 100
weapons 177, 183, 184
weather 38, 39
weaver birds 119
webs 145
wet temperate climate 39
whales 84, 95, 99, 104, 105
whistling swan 115
white stars 19
widow spiders 144
wildebeest 109
wind 44, 45
wind power 45
wind turbines 45
winter 41
wolves 99, 112, 113
wombats 111
worms 133

X

X-rays 61

Y

years 40
yellow-bellied sea snake 87

ACKNOWLEDGEMENTS

The publishers would like to thank the following sources for the use of their photographs:

Key t=top, b=bottom, l=left, r=right, c=centre

COVER (all Shutterstock.com) FRONT (atom) Sashkin, (tiger) Eric Isselee, (toucan) Braam Collins; SPINE (Earth) Alex Staroseltsev, (stag beetle) ethylalkohol; BACK (dinosaur) DM7

Dreamstime 3(br) & 52 Silverstore; 35(cr) Paul Hakimata

Fotolia 33(tl) .shock, (cr) John Saxenian, (br) Melissa Schalke; 37(br) Alexander Zotov; 61(cr) 2happy; 97(cr) rkwphotography; 99(t, third from l) filtv; 109(tr) Vibe Images; 123(cr) javarman; 127(bl) fivespots; 147(tr) Wong Sze Fei

iStockphoto.com 7(cr) janrysavy; 17(cr) wynnter; 65(cr) Brady Willette; 69(cr) IMPALASTOCK; 84(b) micheldenijs; 120(b) RichLindie; 131(tr) hilton123

NASA 8 NASA Jet Propulsion Laboratory (NASA–JPL); 9(cr) NASA/SDO; 13(tr) NASA/ESA/STScI/AURA, (br) ESA/NASA; 20–21 NASA–JPL; 21(tl) NASA Marshall Space Flight Center (NASA–MSFC); 23(tr) NASA Headquarters – Greatest Images of NASA (NASA–HQ–GRIN)

Shutterstock.com 13(bl) MarcelClemens, (cr) Creativemarc; 23(br) Action Sports Photography; 25(tr) Tyler Boyes, (cr) michal812, (br) Tyler Boyes; 29(tl) Alexandr Zyryanov, (tr) Andrey Popov, (cr) Jakub Cejpek; 31(tl) Christian Vinces, (tr) Nataliya Hora, (cr) arindambanerjee; 32(bl) Mogens Trolle; 33(cl) Qba from Poland; 34(l) VLADJ55; 35(br) al coroza; 36(l) Michael Klenetsky; 37(tr) mountainpix, (cr) Lee Prince; 38(tl) apdesign, (cl) Asaf Eliason, (bl) szefei; 39(l, t–b) Oleg Znamenskiy, John De Bord, kkaplin, PHB.cz (Richard Semik), sima, Sergey Toronto, (tr) haveseen, (cr) Asaf Eliason, (br) Brian Lasenby; 40(b) artjazz, (t) Mark Bridger; 41(bl) S.Borisov, (tl) Michael Macsuga, (tr) jan kranendonk, (cr) IM_photo; 42(l) Mirec; 43(tr) Serg64, (cr) elen_studio, (br) Sergey Sergeev; 45(tl) Andrew Zarivny, (tr) Brian Nolan, (cr) B747; 46 kornilov007; 47(bl) Sam DCruz, (bc) Marcin Pawinski, (tr) pasphotography, (cr) livingcanvas; 48–49 jabiru; 49(tl) Songquan Deng, (tr) Barnaby Chambers, (cr) Pablo Scapinachis; 50–51 Deymos.HR; 53(bl) bioraven, (cl) robodread, (br) Chiyacat; 54(cr) Pressmaster, (br) Jennifer Griner; 55(cr) Peter Gudella, (br) SergiyN; 56 vadim kozlovsky; 57(tr) revers, (br) arosoft; 58(b) Ray Hub; 59(tr) Smileus, (cr) dslaven, (br) Kodda; 60(bl) Sebastian Crocker; 61(tl) Hywit Dimyadi; 62 ifong; 63(tl) Viktorus, (bl) Denys Prykhodov, (tr) Zhukov Oleg, (cr) Benko Zsolt, (br) ayazad; 64 Jaggat Rashidi; 65(tl) miker, (bl) Mike Flippo, (tr) rezachka, (br) Christian Mueller; 73(cr) Kostyantyn Ivanyshen; 77(cr); 83(br) Mana Photo; 85(tr) Armin Rose, (cr) Willyam Bradberry; 86 Sergey Uryadnikov; 87(bl) Meister Photos, (tr) Alexey Stiop, (cr) Rich Carey, (br) Matthew W Keefe; 90–91 Specta; 90(b) Eugene Sim; 91(tl) Jim Agronick, (cr) holbox; 93(cl) David Thyberg, (cr) ECOSTOCK; 94 IrinaK; 95(tl) nice_pictures, (bl) Katherine Worzalla, (cr) Vasik Olga; 97(br) Tania Thomson; 99(tl, l–r) Meawpong3405, creativex, (cl) Donna Heatfield, (tr) Michael Sheehan, (br) Eric Gevaert; 101(tr) Liquid Productions, LLC, (cr) alanf; 102 Incredible Arctic; 103(tr) Vladimir Melnik, (cr) samsem, (br) nialat; 105(bl) Marcelo Sanchez, (tr) Jo Crebbin, (cr) Four Oaks, (br) Xavier Marchant; 107(tr) Ammit Jack; 108 muznabutt; 109(tl) Hedrus, (bl) wacpan, (cr) EcoPrint; 111(tl) Henk Paul, (bl) javarman, (tr) My Good Images, (cr) Karel Gallas, (br) Robyn Butler; 112 Richard Seeley; 113(tr) Ron Hilton, (cr) Debbie Aird Photography; 114(tl) Steve Byland, (b) wizdata; 115(bl) Sue McDonald, (tr) Marcin Sylwia Ciesielski, (cr) John Carnemolla, (br) David Evison; 116(cr) Mary Beth Charles; 117(tl) Ewan Chesser, (bl) Eric Isselee, (tr) Stargazer, (cr) Footage.Pro; 118 Kane513; 119(tl) Johan Swanepoel, (tr) M.Camerin, (cr) Florian Andronache; 120 Rich Lindie; 121(tl) Arto Hakola, (bl) Daniel-Alvarez, (cr) Milan M Jurkovic, (br) Michael E. Miller; 122(tl) aabeele; 123(tl) Karel Gallas, (bl) Joe Gough, (tr) Sari ONeal, (br) Villiers Steyn; 125(tr) Colin Edwards Wildside, (cr) wim claes, (br) Justin Black; 126(l) dashingstock; 127(l) worldswildlifewonders, (tr) worldswildlifewonders, (cr) Eduardo Rivero, (br) Sergey Uryadnikov; 128 Footage.Pro; 129(t) Rob McKay, (tr) Jack Cronkhite, (cr) Francis BossÃ©, (br) Martin Fowler; 130(l) BogdanBoev, (r) Xander Fotografie; 131(tl) Borislav Borisov, (bl) Mogens Trolle, (cr) MarclSchauer, (br) Tania Thomson; 132(t) dcb, (b) Tobik; 133(bl) Dusty Cline, (tr) TTstudio, (br) Matthew Cole; 135(tl) irin-k, (tr) Karel Gallas, (cr) Kletr, (br) Volkov Alexey; 137(cr) epsylon_lyrae; 139(bl) alslutsky, (tr) jps, (cr) Alexey Stiop, (br) Smit; 140–141 alslutsky; 141(tl) kurt_G, (tr) Anton Balazh, (cr) Cosmin Manci; 142 Nick Stubbs; 143(tl) Dr. Morley Read, (br) vblinov; 144(bl) Damian Herde; 146(bl) Vinicius Tupinamba; 147(bl) Pan Xunbin; 154–155 WitR; 155(cr) Nestor Noci; 167(tl) Viacheslav Lopatin

Every effort has been made to acknowledge the source and copyright holder of each picture.
Miles Kelly Publishing apologizes for any unintentional errors or omissions.